# THE
# ABERHART
# SUMMER

# THE ABERHART SUMMER

## CONNI MASSING

Based on the novel by Bruce Allen Powe

Edited by Anne Nothof

Prairie Play Series: 17/Series Editor, Diane Bessai

NEWEST PRESS

**Canadian Cataloguing in Publication Data**

Massing, Conni L. (Conni Louise), 1958–
The Aberhart summer

(Prairie play series)
A play.
Based on the novel with the same title by Bruce Allen Powe.
ISBN 1-896300-40-5

I. Powe, Bruce, 1925– . Aberhart summer. II. Title. III. Series.
PS8576.A793A7 1999a    C812'.54    C99-911280-5
PR9199.3.M393A72 1999a

Editor for the Press: Anne Nothof    Series editor: Diane Bessai
Cover and book design: Bob Young
Cover photograph: Trudie Lee (Edward Bélanger as Babe Roothe)

NeWest Press acknowledges the support of the Canada Council for the Arts for our publishing program. We also acknowledge the financial support of the Government of Canada through the Book Publishing Industry Development Program (BPIDP) for our publishing activities.

THE CANADA COUNCIL | LE CONSEIL DES ARTS
FOR THE ARTS | DU CANADA
SINCE 1957 | DEPUIS 1957

Canadian   Patrimoine
Heritage   canadien

Canadä

Photographs have been reproduced with the kind permission of Trudie Lee. Author photo courtesy of Robert van Schaik.

Based on the novel *The Aberhart Summer* by Bruce Allen Powe first published 1983, copyright B. A. Powe, c/o Beverley Slopen, Beverley Slopen Literary Agency, 131 Bloor Street West, Suite 711, Toronto, Ontario M5S 1S3.

Every effort has been made to obtain permission for material used in this book. If there is an omission or error the author and publisher would be grateful to be so informed.

Printed and bound in Canada

NeWest Publishers Limited
Suite 201, 8540-109 Street
Edmonton, Alberta T6G 1E6

For Ed and Vi

# CONTENTS

# FOREWORD
## by Stephen Heatley

It wasn't until Kevin Kruchkywich as Doug Sayers uttered the words, "That was a long time ago, though, and I'm alright now," and the lights faded to black on opening night of *The Aberhart Summer* at Alberta Theatre Projects, that I finally believed that the show would actually see an audience. My response may sound a little over dramatic, but this project had so many false starts, I guess I was a little gun-shy.

I first read and fell in love with the novel on which it is based—Bruce Allen Powe's *The Aberhart Summer*—in 1984. I had become hooked on Alberta's political history and was on the lookout for anything that had to do with the rise of Bible Bill Aberhart, arguably Alberta's most colourful politician. At the time I was the Artistic Director of Edmonton's Theatre Network, and we were preparing a production called *Is Nothing Socred Anymore?* which explored Alberta's penchant for crowning its premiers. (It had happened with the Liberals in 1905, the United Farmers in 1921, the Socreds in 1935, and the Progressive Conservatives in 1971.) I was fascinated with the fact that these parties absolutely dominated their respective legislatures, but when the public finally became disenchanted, the first three were literally obliterated from the political landscape! For me, Bruce's novel beautifully mixed the "big" story of the rise of Social Credit in 1935 with the smaller story of the adolescent boys in Mill Creek. I knew that I wanted to see *The Aberhart Summer* on stage someday.

In 1991 I introduced Theatre Network's playwright-in-residence, Conni Massing, to the novel and asked her if she would consider adapting it for the stage. I knew Conni would be perfect for the job since she has Alberta soil in her pores and a healthy dollop of Social Credit in her Central Alberta family background. She agreed enthusiastically and we began plans for our masterpiece. I wanted to experiment with the process of adapting a novel into dramatic form, so ten actors, a designer, and Conni, Bruce, and I all met together in November 1991 to explore the dramatic potential of the novel. This workshop was designed to provide the inspiration for the playwright to begin the daunting task of adaptation. The three amazing days that ensued were both exciting and inspiring—everything I had hoped for with such an exceptional array of talent. Conni took our discoveries away, created a first draft, and we put the work on the playbill for the end of the 1992–93 Theatre Network season. After a very exciting workshop of this first draft, which included the input of a sound designer and costume designer, Conni began work on the second draft.

At this point, the process came screeching to a halt. The Theatre Network board determined that the theatre couldn't afford a production of this scale and decided that the production would be cancelled for that season. I argued against their decision but to no avail, so I felt I had no other choice than to resign. After eleven and a half years as Artistic Director, this was a very difficult personal decision.

Ten months later, Theatre Network appointed Ben Henderson as its new Artistic Director. Ben immediately programmed *The Aberhart Summer* in his first season and invited me to direct. We held another workshop in the fall of 1993, and Conni and I continued to work on the script with a gifted group of University of Alberta acting students through that autumn in preparation for a March production. In January, a rumour began to circulate throughout the Edmonton theatre community that Theatre Network was in financial distress, and that the production would again be "postponed." I couldn't believe it! Edmonton actor, Jeff Haslam, began referring to the play as "Edmonton's longest running gag." The rumour turned out to be true; we all accepted our payout and agreed not to come to work and not to produce the play. Ben Henderson, however, did take the script to the summer theatre he was running in Fort Macleod, and produced it there with an enthusiastic group of young actors in the summer of 1994. I gave up hope of ever having the chance to direct it.

Well, I almost gave up hope. In 1998, I was working as Associate Artistic Director to Duncan McIntosh at the Citadel Theatre. He had made a commitment to produce "new works of scale" on the main stages of that major player in Edmonton theatre, and had put me in charge of finding and developing these works. Aha! I suggested *The Aberhart Summer* (warily), and he expressed interest. We did a reading of it in June 1998, and he was genuinely excited about the play. At the same time, Bob White, Artistic Associate at Alberta Theatre Projects in Calgary, was visiting Edmonton. Over a "smart brunch," he suggested that we co-produce the work, beginning with a production as part of Global playRites, ATP's annual festival of world premières. Duncan agreed, and I was assigned to direct on behalf of the Citadel. Everything was in place for a Calgary production in 1998–99, and FINALLY, an Edmonton production in 1999–2000. I happily went on vacation for a month. By the time I arrived back in Edmonton in late August of 1998, Duncan and the Citadel had suddenly agreed to part ways, and it looked like the whole scenario was about to repeat itself. Would the city of Edmonton ever get to see this story about itself on one of its stages?

Well, everything has turned out fine. Bob Baker was appointed as the new Artistic Director of the Citadel—its first Edmonton-born artistic leader—and he immediately made a commitment to producing new plays about Alberta by Albertans. *The Aberhart Summer* was included in his first playbill and, in fact, will be the first play to breathe life at the Citadel in the new millennium. The fact that Bob's grandfather, Floyd Baker, had been an MLA in Aberhart's first government in 1935 didn't hurt matters.

It is in this light, then, that I warmly welcome you to this wonderful story and Conni Massing's fine theatrical adaptation of it. Getting to the Edmonton opening has been quite a ride!

# INTRODUCTION
## by Conni Massing

When Stephen Heatley asked me to read Bruce Powe's wonderful book during the spring of 1991 as a possible source for a stage adaptation at Theatre Network, I was immediately struck by the theatrical possibilities of the story. I also fell in love with the novel's treatment of a couple of great Alberta traditions: dramatic weather and peculiar politics. Both can provoke and humble and deceive us. Both exert undue influence over the lives of the characters in *The Aberhart Summer*.

In the fall of that year, Stephen gathered together a company which included ten actors, a designer, me, and Bruce Powe for our first exploration of the material. I chose passages from the book that seemed to have dramatic potential, and for three days we played with story-telling techniques, presentational styles, and theatrical angles on the novel's imagery. It was a bit like an advanced university theatre class, in all the best ways. I was optimistic and excited, and completely overwhelmed at the scope of what we were doing. Still, if anyone had told me on the day we began the workshop (November 23, 1991) that it would be exactly seven years before we gathered around the table to begin rehearsal for the professional première of the play, I would have thought them insane or at least terribly pessimistic.

The play began to evolve (with the help of a grant from the Alberta Foundation for the Arts to support me while I wrote), and another full-scale workshop of the first draft in the spring of 1992. The play was scheduled for production in the spring of 1993—and that's when the first storm blew in. In a precursor of what has now become almost commonplace in Canadian theatre, a struggle between the artistic director and the general manager of the theatre to influence the board of directors was won hands-down by the general manager. The Theatre Network board, acting on the advice of the general manager, decided that the theatre couldn't afford to do the show. Stephen quit, the actors' contracts were paid out, and the brochure advertising the upcoming season became birdcage liner.

I was moderately devastated. Obviously I wanted to continue the work with Stephen and the actors, then see the play in front of an audience. But I also saw in the show's cancellation an unceremonious end to my relationship with Theatre Network, where I'd been "in residence" for five years. No one had asked me to leave, but it seemed pointless to stay since the focus of my work there had been the creative partnership with Stephen. The new artistic director, wishing to resuscitate the badly damaged reputation of the theatre, scheduled the play for production the following year. I don't think any of us really believed it would happen. And it didn't. The play went on to have two other near-productions before the "curse" was broken in 1994 by a semi-professional production in Fort Macleod, at Great West Theatre. The company of young actors (all but one of them under 25), did a swirling, high energy rendition of the play, and a part of me thought, "Well that's it—at least it saw the light of day."

When a markedly different version of the play finally did go into rehearsal in 1998 for a co-production between Alberta Theatre Projects and Edmonton's Citadel Theatre, I must confess that I was extremely grateful that the play's development had taken a different course. Not only are ATP and the Citadel larger venues with more resources to put toward production, but the script is a deeper, clearer piece of work all these years later. Maybe the play's theme of returning to old hurts and haunts has more meaning for me now.

I feel truly blessed to have had such a harmonious relationship with the author of the novel during the development of this piece. Bruce was studiously "hands-off" during the sessions he was present for, but extremely conscientious when asked for feedback. I think it's been a mutually beneficial relationship. Bruce once told me that the experience of watching the actors work with his material inspired him to go back to his own writing. For me, there were many other benefits to the connection with Bruce besides the obvious inspiration of the source material. I'll never forget the trudge through the Mill Creek area (the setting for the book and Bruce's childhood turf). Bruce led the tour, with actors, director and playwright following close behind—the whole procession occasionally coming to a halt so Bruce could re-light his pipe. It was almost possible to see the old neighbourhood as Bruce described the heat waves, streetcar routes, and semi-rural surroundings of his youth, even though we were now shivering in the cold, surrounded by dirty snow and new terra cotta-coloured real estate. The hand-drawn map that Bruce gave us that day became one of our production artifacts.

Perhaps best of all, I felt that a connection to Bruce was also a connection to the central character of the story, Doug Sayers. While I'm not suggesting that the novel is completely autobiographical, there's more than a little similarity between the two men: the wry humour, the basic humanity, and the perspective gained from long experience. That perspective became my way into the material during this last rewrite of the play. How do we discover and then judge the events that have shaped us as we look back on our lives? And how do we make peace with regrettable decisions, and the colder, crueler aspects of ourselves?

It has been a long and very interesting journey to get to the point of actually seeing this play on stage, with a great deal of weather and politics encountered along the way, as well as a great many people I want to thank. The play has benefited from the assistance of the following individuals and organizations: the Alberta Foundation for the Arts, Theatre Network, Great West Theatre, the Citadel Theatre, Alberta Theatre Projects, Ben Henderson, David Mann, and the cast of both the ATP production and the Great West Theatre production. The play was workshopped at the Banff PlayRites Colony—a partnership between the Canada Council, the Banff Centre for the Arts, and Alberta Theatre Projects.

Finally, special thanks to Bruce Powe for allowing me to muck around with his novel, and to Stephen Heatley, who introduced me to the book and has been my partner on this project and many others.

*The Aberhart Summer* was first produced by Great West Theatre in Fort Macleod, Alberta in July 1994, with the following cast:

| | |
|---|---|
| Doug Sayers | *Kevin Kruchkywich* |
| Albert Roothe/Neil Cawner/Passenger #1/Old Man 1/Bar Patron | |
| | *Scott Lancastle* |
| Hamilton "Babe" Roothe/Vic Bell/Juryman/Examiner #3/Bar Patron/Mover | |
| | *Geoff Lacny* |
| Mr. Thorpe/Billy Cawner/Policeman/Examiner #1/Seelheim/Bar Patron | |
| | *George Szilagyi* |
| Peter Thorpe/Mr. Sayers/Crown Counsel Haddon/Heckler/Bar Manager/ | |
| Man 2 | *Tony Eyamie* |
| Norman Fetterman/School Official/Announcer/Howson | |
| | *Craig Wademan* |
| William Aberhart/Coroner/Bar Patron/Old Man 2/Man 1 | |
| | *Grahame Renyk* |
| Mrs. Sayers/Mabel/Passenger #2/Examiner #2/Bar Patron/Lymburn | |
| | *Rhonda NuGent* |
| Mrs. Fetterman/Jean Cullen/Doctor/Barker/Bar Patron | |
| | *Kelly Hubka* |
| Mrs. Roothe/Diane Thorpe/Duggan/Bar Patron | |
| | *Sharla Matkin* |
| Director | *David Mann* |
| Designer | *Robert Shannon* |
| Musical Director | *Trudi Ellis* |
| Stage Manager | *Allan Bassil* |
| Assistant Stage Manager | *Shauna Murphy* |
| Technical Director | *David Gibson* |
| Assistant Technical Director | *Sandra Train* |

A revised version of *The Aberhart Summer* premièred as a co-production between Alberta Theatre Projects and Edmonton's Citadel Theatre as part of playRites '99 in Calgary, Alberta in January 1999, with the following cast:

| | |
|---|---|
| Babe Roothe | *Edward Bélanger* |
| Diane Thorpe/Jean Cullen | *Tara Hughes* |
| Albert Roothe | *Christopher Hunt* |
| Doug Sayers | *Kevin Kruchkywich* |
| Mrs. Roothe/Mrs. Fetterman | *Nicola Lipman* |
| Peter Thorpe | *Brian Marler* |
| Mr. Thorpe | *Allan Morgan* |
| Norman Fetterman | *Philip Warren Sarsons* |
| Mr. Sayers | *Kent Staines* |
| Mrs. Sayers | *Maureen Thomas* |
| William Aberhart | *William Webster* |

| | |
|---|---|
| Director | *Stephen Heatley* |
| Production Stage Manager | *Dianne Goodman* |
| Stage Manager | *Cheryl L. Hoover* |
| Assistant Stage Manager | *Rebecca Eamon* |
| Junior Apprentice | *Geneviève Bédard* |
| Set Designer | *Scott Reid* |
| Costume Designer | *Judith Bowden* |
| Lighting Designer | *Brian Pincott* |
| Assistant Designer | *Kim Stewart* |
| Composer | *Allan Rae* |
| Production Dramaturge | *Bill Glassco* |

# THE ABERHART SUMMER

## THE CHARACTERS

**Doug Sayers**, as an adult and age 15

**Mrs. Sayers**/Streetcar Passenger #2/Examiner #2

**Mr. Sayers**/Streetcar Conductor/Heckler/Bible College
Official/Policeman/German-Canadian Picnic Politicians

**Norm Fetterman**/Doctor

**Mrs. Fetterman**/Mrs. Roothe/Streetcar Passenger #1

**Babe Roothe**/Barker/ Mover/Patient

**Albert Roothe**

**Jean Cullen**/Diane Thorpe/Neil Cawner/Child

**Peter Thorpe**/Adult

**Mr. Thorpe**/Woodwards Floorwalker/Examiner #1

**William Aberhart**/Vic Bell/Coroner

## PRODUCTION NOTES

The characters and the Chorus may be performed by ten to twelve actors.
The members of the Chorus may speak as a group or as individual voices
(*various*) or characters.

*The Aberhart Summer* is a memory play of Edmonton in which various time
periods are recalled, primarily of the summer of 1935, against the backdrop
of William Aberhart's election sweep of Alberta. The shifts in specific times
and locations are fluid.

# ACT ONE

## SCENE 1

*The action takes place on and around an old-fashioned wooden grandstand, the underside facing the audience. An adult Doug enters and observes a silence before he speaks.*

**Doug:** This morning a piece of shrapnel worked its way through my skin while I was shaving. God knows how much is still in there—my little souvenir from the last days of the war. My mother used to say you could float me in a pond and I'd point due north, like a compass.

*Doug walks down the sidewalk.*

**Doug:** She died last week with an overdue library book in her lap and an overflowing ashtray by her side, both reproaches to my neglect. I just closed up her house here in Mill Creek. Salvaged . . . a few dishes, some photo albums, books, and one of my old soft caps. *Pulls it out of his pocket, tries it on.*

Doesn't fit anymore. I've loaded up the car and now . . . I can't quite leave. Maybe because I know I'll never be back. *A beat, then he gestures toward a "house."* The old Fetterman place.

*Doug stops and observes as Norm Fetterman (14) appears, struggling to escape the grasp of Mrs. Fetterman, who has him by the ear. Norm hops around in a circle and yelps piteously.*

**Norm:** Ow-ow-ow-ow!

**Doug:** My old buddy Norm Fetterman.

**Mrs. Fetterman:** I'll give you something to cry about!

**Doug:** During the war he won a Military Medal for bravery.

**Norm:** *As he struggles free.* Mom!

*Norm runs to the Sayers house and raps on the door. Mrs. Sayers, carrying a library book and smoking a cigarette, shuffles to the door at the same time as Mr. Sayers approaches from the opposite direction, face buried in a newspaper.*

**Norm:** Morning, Mr. and Mrs. Sayers. Is Dougie . . . ?

**Mr. Sayers:** Uh-huh.

*Mr. Sayers wanders off.*

**Mrs. Sayers:** Come on in. Your mother feeling better?

**Norm:** Guess so.

**Doug:** My mother always knew everything about everybody.

**Mrs. Sayers:** *To Doug.* Don't be smart.

**Doug:** She wasn't a gossip, exactly, but intelligence about the neighborhood seemed to find its way to her.

*Mrs. Sayers exits.*

**Doug:** On the other side of our house was the Roothe place. The house is so different I have trouble visualizing my friend Babe again, in his last summer. Slouching out the door to take command of our endless days of idleness, or to torment his older brother Albert, who was busy changing the world in the name of a new political party called Social Credit.

*Babe (15) comes to the door and blocks the exit as Albert (26) tries to dodge past him, doing up a tie. Albert grabs Babe by the shirt just as Mrs. Roothe comes to the door, smiling sweetly. She hands Albert a lunch bag.*

**Mrs. Roothe:** Off you go now.

**Doug:** *Sarcastic.* Atta boy, Albert.

*Mrs. Roothe and Albert melt into the shadows. Babe stays behind. He follows Doug toward the Thorpe house, watching Doug with an amused air.*

**Doug:** Next door to Babe, old man Headley kept his horses in a barn at the back of his property. On the other side of Headleys was the smallest of the houses on our street. The Thorpes lived there, always frantically praying and hollering about heavenly wrath.

*Doug stops in front of the Thorpe house.*

Diane Thorpe, perfect and unattainable as a movie star. And Pete, her brother, missing all these years, whose only weapon against our cruelty was his talent for mimicry.

*Diane and Pete sit at a table. Diane is reading. Pete is restless.*

**Pete:** *A convincing imitation of "The Shadow" radio voice.* What evil lurks in the hearts of men? The Shadow knows!

*Mr. Thorpe enters. Pete cowers.*

**Mr. Thorpe:** Peter!

**Doug:** Old man Thorpe. Loving father and one of the most ruthless tax collectors the city ever employed.

**Mr. Thorpe:** Have you been listening to a radio again?

**Pete:** N-no. N-no!

*Mr. Thorpe exits. Diane looks up from her book to see Babe staring at her.*

*Doug watches them for a moment, until Diane exits. Pete stays behind and stares at Doug.*

**Doug:** *Shaking his head at the memory.* Pete . . .

*Pete exits. Doug tries to leave again. From behind him he hears . . .*

**Babe:** Hiya, Dougie.

*Doug stops dead in his tracks.*

**Doug:** I really should get going.

*Babe laughs.*

**Babe:** Aww, Dougie . . .

*Doug slowly turns toward Babe, who is grinning.*

**Doug:** Jesus . . . look at you.

**Babe:** Wanna go to a picnic?

**Doug:** Babe . . .

**Babe:** I'm going to the picnic.

**Doug:** Babe—look, I'm sorry—I just didn't know!

*There are stirrings in the background as the Neighborhood Chorus drifts in. A couple of organizers erect a sign—"Northern Alberta Social Credit Picnic."*

**Chorus:** Saturday, July 6, 1935. Northern Alberta Social Credit Picnic.

**Doug:** *To audience.* Maybe you wouldn't have known either.

*Doug is caught up in the picnic preparations. Children play tag on the stage. They're pursued by a sweaty chaperon, engaged to keep them in line until it's time to perform. Someone else starts to work his way through the audience, handing out brochures and saying: "Aberhart will be speaking today . . . two o'clock." An Edmonton Chamber of Commerce type bursts in the back door and tries to hand out "The Dangers of Aberhart's Money Policy," but he is soon tackled by a couple of Aberhart lieutenants who frog-march him out of the theatre. He protests loudly—"it's a free country—people deserve to know the facts,"* etc.

*Babe removes Doug's glasses and places the soft cap on his head—it "fits" now. He gives Doug a little shove.*

**Babe:** *Impatient.* Dougie!

*Babe exits.*


## SCENE 2

*Doug (15) approaches Mrs. Sayers.*

**Doug:** Could I have a quarter to go to the Social Credit picnic at the Ex?

**Mrs. Sayers:** What makes you think I've got a quarter to spare?

**Doug:** And, uh, streetcar tickets.

**Mrs. Sayers:** Can't you find something else to do?

**Doug:** Well Babe says Albert says there's a carnival going on up there. It's an all-day picnic.

**Mrs. Sayers:** So you'll want some sandwiches, too?

**Doug:** Guess so.

*Mr. Sayers enters, reading a newspaper.*

**Mr. Sayers:** Where is it you think you're going?

**Doug:** The Social Credit picnic.

**Mr. Sayers:** Has Albert talked you two into going because they want all the warm bodies they can get to hear Aberhart? Is that it?

**Doug:** Nah, Albert's got no hold on Babe. Babe just figured the picnic would be something to do, good for a laugh.

*Mr. Sayers grunts, exits.*

**Doug:** Norm Fetterman's going. His mom's making sandwiches for him. *Beat.* And they might lose their house.

**Mrs. Sayers:** Now who told you that? She's just a little behind on her taxes.

**Doug:** You think old Thorpe'll let her off?

**Mrs. Sayers:** You know all the gossip, don't you?

**Doug:** I live here, don't I?

**Mrs. Sayers:** *Starts to hand Doug a quarter, then stops.* Don't be smart. I bet you Mrs. Fetterman doesn't have a quarter.

**Doug:** We'll go dibs. I'll make sure Norm gets a pop.

**Mrs. Sayers:** I'm not sure your father really wants you going.

**Doug:** Tell him I'm going as a spy.

**Mrs. Sayers:** *After a beat.* Well don't do anything dumb.

**Doug:** We won't.

*A last warning look before she turns away. Doug looks out the window.*

**Doug:** Here comes Mrs. Fetterman now. Coming to make her report.

*Mrs. Sayers shoots Doug a look, pretends to swat at him. Doug grins.*


**SCENE 3**

*Norm and Doug run toward the streetcar. Chorus holds up a banner that reads: "Special—Exhibition."*

**Doug:** You're in the clear. Old man Thorpe's given your mom a couple more weeks to pay her taxes.

**Norm:** How'd you know that?

**Doug:** *With a shrug.* Maybe I heard it on the radio.

**Norm:** Really?

*Pete Thorpe skulks up.*

**Conductor:** All a-booaard!

*They move on to the streetcar. Pete and Diane Thorpe sit apart from Norm, Doug, and Babe. Other Passengers sit nearby, picnic baskets on their laps.*

**Pete:** Y-you guys going to the picnic?

**Doug:** What do you think?

**Norm:** Yeah, whaddaya think?

*Doug and Norm look at Babe for support. But Babe is staring at Diane, who presses a delicate blue hankie against her forehead to absorb a few beads of sweat.*

**Doug:** Babe? What's with you today anyway?

**Norm:** Yeah, what's up? You smell funny.

**Doug:** Like vanilla extract.

**Babe:** It's aftershave.

**Norm:** *Admiring.* You shave?

**Babe:** Pipe down, alright.

**Doug:** Didya tell Albert we were coming to his picnic?

**Babe:** Naw, I wanted to surprise him.

**Doug:** He'll think you flipped.

**Babe:** *With a shrug.* I wouldn't miss old Abie's speech for the world. I want my twenty-five bucks a month.

**Norm:** The government's gonna give money to kids?

**Babe:** Oh yeah. Every man, woman, child, and household pet.

**Norm:** Pets, too?!

*Norm and Doug look wide-eyed for a moment till Babe laughs. Pete looks at them longingly.*

**Pete:** *As Aberhart.* Now my friends, you're all here to be saved. Give me your souls and I will give you twenty-five dollars a month.

*A couple of the other Passengers react.*

**Passenger #1:** Where's that coming from?

**Passenger #2:** That's Aberhart!

*Pete giggles.*

**Diane:** *Embarrassed.* Peter!

**Pete:** *To Babe.* Wh-what should I do next? Babe?

*But Babe and Diane are staring at each other, frozen.*

**Conductor:** Exhibition Grounds!

*Bodies tumble out of the streetcar. Diane and Babe disappear along with the crowd, leaving Norm and Doug trailing behind.*

**Passenger #2:** *Chasing Pete.* Don't you make fun of Mr. Aberhart!

**Norm:** Hey, Babe? Where'd he go?

**Doug:** Come on. Come on! Babe!

*Doug charges off at a run. Norm follows.*


**SCENE 4**

*The picnic. Doug and Norm spot Mrs. Roothe. Jean is with her.*

**Norm:** Look, there's Mrs. Roothe. She has a picnic basket!

**Mrs. Roothe:** Peanut butter or ham?

**Norm:** Ham, please.

**Doug:** Thanks, Mrs. Roothe.

**Jean:** How are you boys enjoying yourselves?

**Doug:** Fine, thank you, Jean. *Aside to audience.* Albert's girlfriend, Jean Cullen. I always suspected she was bored by all his sweaty politics. I was sure she was secretly longing for me.

**Jean:** Norm?

**Norm:** Uh . . . fine, thank you.

**Jean:** Didn't know you were interested in politics.

**Norm:** We're not.

*Doug elbows Norm. Albert charges up.*

**Doug:** Hey, Albert. You seen Babe?

**Albert:** No.

**Mrs. Roothe:** I thought he was with you lads.

**Doug:** He was with us on the streetcar, then we got here and he disappeared.

**Mrs. Roothe:** I'm sure he'll turn up.

**Albert:** I'm sure he wouldn't miss the program.

**Doug:** No, I bet he wouldn't.

**Albert:** You boys are sticking around for Mr. Aberhart's speech, aren't you?

*Albert stares the boys down. Mrs. Roothe smiles at them and offers another sandwich.*

**Doug:** Yeah, we'll stay.

**Norm:** Yeah sure. These are good sandwiches. They've got more meat in them than the ones that Mrs. Sayers made.

**Doug:** Shhh!

**Albert:** Shush, it's starting now.

*Aberhart moves into position to speak. Four members of the Chorus, playing the "horses," move into position at the starting line for the race.*

**Aberhart:** Ladies and gentlemen. Please join me in a little pleasant speculation about the future of this province. From the Conservative Party Stables, it's a three-year-old gelding called Broken Promise. Wearing the red silk, we have the Liberal Party's favorite, Depression Dora. Limping into position now we have that sad old nag entered by the United Farmers of Alberta, Nervous Nelly. The dark horse, folks, is Social Credit, sired by New Era and Just Reward. And they're off . . . It's

Broken Promise in the lead, then Depression Dora. Nervous Nelly. Social Credit is trailing, folks.

*The crowd responds with a groan. The competitors make a great show of jockeying for position.*

**Aberhart:** But just a second here, just hang on folks. It's a long shot but I think Social Credit is moving up in the field. Gaining ground, gaining ground. This is tremendous!

*They cross the finish line.*

**Aberhart:** It's Social Credit by a country mile! Liberals, place. Conservatives, show. United Farmers of Alberta, also ran.

*Much cheering and jeering. Then the crowd moves into the configuration of a congregation, with Aberhart as the minister.*

**All:** *Singing.* What a friend we have in Jesus,
All our sins and griefs to bear!
What a privilege to carry
Everything to God in prayer!
O what peace we often forfeit,
O what needless pain we bear,
All because we do not carry
Everything to God in prayer.

*The Chorus continues to hum underneath the following.*

**Aberhart:** You remain in the Depression because of a shortage of purchasing power, imposed by the banking system. Social Credit offers you the remedy. *Pause.* Twenty-five dollars per month for every Albertan. If you have not suffered enough, it is your God-given right to suffer more. But if you wish to elect your own representatives to implement the remedy, this is your only way out.

*Albert leaps to his feet.*

**Albert:** The only way out!

**Aberhart:** Our struggle is like a deep-sea diver with a devil-fish. Our battle is a terrific strangling combat with the money octopus. But we still have one hand free with which to strike: to mark our ballot on election day. Let us strike, then, with all our might at this hideous monster that is sucking the very life-blood from our people!

*A roar goes up from the crowd. They sing "Oh God Our Help in Ages Past" as they leave the picnic.*

**Chorus:** *Singing.* O God, our help in ages past,
Our hope for years to come,
Our shelter from the stormy blast,
And our eternal home!

*Albert remains still as the procession files past him. As Aberhart leaves, he shakes Albert's hand and whispers something in his ear. Albert is stunned.*

**Jean:** Albert. What'd he say?

**Albert:** Maybe next time.

**Doug:** That's when Albert took the hook. After that it seemed like he never gave a damn for Babe or anyone else.


## SCENE 5

*The Sayers household. We hear the last of the hymn as though it is being broadcast. Mr. Sayers goes to the radio and turns it off.*

**Mr. Sayers:** That's enough of Bible Bill and his holy rollers.

**Doug:** He talked to Albert.

**Mr. Sayers:** *To Mrs. Sayers.* Albert was considered as a candidate by the Social Credit's Central Committee. Word came back he was still too young but maybe next time . . .

**Mrs. Sayers:** Funny. Babe's the natural politician in the family. A regular Pied Piper. But Albert wants it so badly . . .

**Doug:** Albert wants to be a politician?

**Mr. Sayers:** He sure does. But first the UFA has to call an election. Do you know what UFA stands for, Doug?

**Doug:** Underwear Freeloaders of Alberta—

**Mr. Sayers:** Very funny. United Farmers of Alberta.

**Doug:** *Joining in.* United Farmers of Alberta. But when Social Credit wins, we all get money.

**Mr. Sayers:** No, Dougie. I don't believe it'll ever happen. Aberhart's just a smart politician manipulating a lot of desperate people.

*Mrs. Roothe enters.*

**Mr. Sayers:** Morning, Mrs. Roothe.

**Mrs. Roothe:** He's gone. Is he over here with you, Dougie?

**Doug:** What?

**Mrs. Roothe:** Babe. He slipped out his bedroom window. Took the screen right off. Now, why would he do a thing like that?

**Doug:** Gee, I don't know, Mrs. Roothe. Last time I saw Babe was on Saturday when he ditched Norm and me. And we never called for him yesterday.

**Mr. Sayers:** How come?

**Doug:** We were mad at him for taking off on us. Never saw him yesterday at all.

*Albert enters the Sayers' kitchen, dressed for work.*

**Albert:** I looked up and down the street, there's no sign of him.

**Mr. Sayers:** If you want to stay, I can tell them at work you'll be late.

**Albert:** No, he'll show up. I'll call you at noon, Mom. No point calling the police yet.

**Mr. Sayers:** Don't want the publicity, Albert?

**Albert:** I just don't think there's any reason to worry yet.

**Mr. Sayers:** Okay. Alley Oop.

*Albert and Mr. Sayers exit.*

**Mrs. Sayers:** Why don't you round up a gang and go look for Babe?

**Mrs. Roothe:** Would you, Dougie?

**Doug:** Sure thing. Don't know where, but we'll take a gander.


## SCENE 6

*"Shadow" laugh is heard offstage.*

**Pete:** *Off.* Who knows what evil lurks in the hearts of men?

*Doug picks up Norm in front of his house. Pete enters, does the Shadow laugh again, then lurks shyly, waiting for approval.*

**Doug:** Babe's taken a powder. We're sposed to look for him.

**Norm:** *Jerking his head towards Pete.* Looks like we got company.

**Pete:** *Radio voice as "Amos and Andy."* You fellas doin' anything?

**Doug:** Naw.

**Norm:** Let's go down and check the ruins.

**Doug:** Fine with me.

*Diane enters and tries to get Pete's attention.*

**Norm:** *Elbowing Doug.* Psst! It's Diane.

**Diane:** Pete . . .

**Pete:** *"Amos and Andy."* Me an da Kingfish, we has a scheme.

**Doug:** Hi, Diane.

*Diane ignores them.*

**Diane:** Papa says to come in.

**Pete:** *Doing Diane.* Papa says to come in.

*Doug rolls his eyes, starts to move away. Norm laughs. Pete is delighted. Diane exits.*

**Doug:** *To Norm.* Alley Oop.

**Pete:** *"Amos and Andy."* What parts are you young whippersnappers headin'?

**Doug:** We're going down to the creek to see if we can find Babe.

**Pete:** *His own voice.* W-what d-do you m-mean, find him?

**Doug:** He's gone, done a bunk.

**Pete:** G-gone where?

**Doug:** If we knew we wouldn't be looking for him. Maybe Billy Cawner and that bunch have seen him. Yeah, maybe we'll ask the Cawners.

**Pete:** C-Cawners!

*Pete runs back into his own yard.*

**Norm:** That settles his hash. *A pause, worried.* We're not really going to talk to the Cawners, are we?

**Doug:** Why, are you scared?

**Norm:** Babe said they held Sid Webb's little brother down and fed him Exlax.

*The Neighborhood Chorus emerges from the shadows. Mrs. Sayers starts to hang up wash.*

**Doug:** I heard they held a gun to his head.

**Norm:** Babe said if we go near their caves, we've had it.

**Mrs. Sayers:** I'd like to know what's in those caves.

*Mrs. Roothe comes out and leans over her fence, watching Mrs. Sayers hang up her wash.*

**Doug:** Car parts and furniture and jewelry.

**Mr. Thorpe:** Stolen goods!

**Mr. Sayers:** *To Mr. Thorpe.* They're like rooms carved right into the side of Mill Creek Ravine. Bloody clever.

**Doug & Norm:** Babe says they have an old mattress in there and for two bits you can do it with one of the Cawner's girl cousins.

**Norm:** You can do it!

**Mr. Thorpe:** Sinning, heathenous . . .

**Pete:** Th-they have a pack of big dogs.

**Mrs. Roothe:** Neil Cawner, Billy Cawner, Joe . . . it's hard to keep track of them all.

**Mrs. Sayers:** He's a remittance man.

**Mrs. Roothe:** She's a drinker.

**Doug & Norm:** Babe says they have bootleg liquor.

*The Chorus moves off.*

**Chorus:** Careful! It's dangerous down there.


## SCENE 7

**Norm:** You really want to check the caves?

**Doug:** Nah, it's too risky.

*Neil Cawner steps out of the shadows, carrying a gun.*

**Neil:** You're right, kid.

**Norm:** Neil Cawner!

**Doug:** Neil! We were just—

**Neil:** Couple of elephants crashing through the bush.

**Doug:** We were just cutting through.

**Neil:** You sure about that?

**Doug:** No—I mean yes. We're sure. Honest.

**Neil:** Make up your mind.

*Doug and Norm run. The Coroner enters and observes.*

**Coroner:** Call Douglas Sayers and Norman Fetterman.

**Doug:** We climbed up the ravine as fast as we could! We ran down the alley . . .

**Norm:** Look—there's Neil!

**Doug:** Come on! Let's cut through McBrides!

**Norm:** Do you think he's chasing us?

**Doug:** Dunno! Yeah!

**Norm:** There's your mom—

**Doug:** Hanging up the wash. Scram!

**Norm:** Duck behind the hedge—around Headley's barn.

**Doug:** Into the side door.

**Chorus:** The barn was dark. Except for small beams of light from empty knotholes. The horse stalls were empty. The air was heavy, gamy, fragrant—

**Norm:** Let's go up top. If Neil comes in, he won't see nothing.

**Doug:** Guy could kill himself on all this harness.

**Norm:** Here. We can sit here.

*Doug and Norm pant with relief. A silence, then:*

**Doug:** What's that noise?

**Norm:** What?

**Doug:** That squeaky, creaky noise.

**Chorus:** The squeaky rubbing of weighted rope on the joist. Like the sound of an old ship taking someone away.

**Norm:** Look . . .

**Doug:** It's dark . . .

**Norm:** Look, it's . . .

**Chorus:** Babe . . .

*Babe is revealed—swinging from a beam. Norm and Doug react to Babe, letting out a yell, then run into the Sayers' backyard.*

**Doug:** Tore into my backyard and got caught up in the wash—

**Norm:** Doug's mom—

**Doug:** Turned and let her cigarette drop from her mouth.

*All three of them freeze for a moment.*

**Doug:** I was the first to shout out what we had found.

*Mrs. Sayers grabs both boys by the arms, plants them firmly on chairs.*

**Mrs. Sayers:** Don't goddamn well move.

*Babe moves downstage and grins. A flash from a camera freezes him in place. A collective groan from the Neighbours, who then gather around a stricken Mrs. Roothe.*

**Mrs. Sayers:** Senseless. So young . . .

**Jean:** He never had a care in the world.

**Mrs. Sayers:** He was a Pied Piper. A natural.

**Albert:** He was secretive. Who knew what he thought . . .

**Mrs. Roothe:** He was a happy boy. Wasn't he . . . ?

**Mr. Thorpe:** Diane. It's the young Roothe boy. He committed suicide in Mr. Headley's barn. Hung himself.

**Diane:** No! No, he wouldn't—

**Mr. Thorpe:** *Dropping to his knees.* Our father who art in heaven . . .

*Diane joins Mr. Thorpe in prayer.*

**Both:** Hallowed be thy name.

*Prayer continues under . . .*

**Various:** How long had he been there?

Why hadn't the horses made a fuss about the smell of death in the barn?

Maybe it happened after Headley left on his rounds.

No note, no letter, no clues?

*Diane and Mr. Thorpe finish praying.*

**Doug:** I had dream after dream about finding a suicide note. A little scrap of paper stuffed into a school exercise book. Or a few lines scrawled on a postcard.

**Babe:** Dear Dougie . . . wish you were here. No heat waves, no cold snaps, just lots of light.

**Doug:** No!

*Chorus of Neighbors escorts Mrs. Roothe off.*

**Chorus:** *Singing.* O God, our help in ages past,
Our hope for years to come,
Our shelter from the stormy blast,
And our eternal home!


## SCENE 8

*The Sayers household. Doug and Norm wait to be interrogated.*

**Doug:** So we're going to get the third degree.

**Norm:** I thought that's what we'd been through. What'll we say?

**Doug:** You figure it out, bud. Suppose they put two and two together, make the connection with the Cawners, that we were on the run from them?

**Norm:** I d-dunno.

**Doug:** Let's get out of here.

**Norm:** How we gonna do that?

**Doug:** I'll pinch some money from Mom's purse.

**Norm:** What are we gonna do?

**Doug:** Come on!

*They make a run for it.*

**Norm:** There's a streetcar. Where are we going to go?

**Doug:** Over town.

*The boys get on the streetcar and take seats.*

**Doug:** Isn't that your mom?

**Norm:** Where?

**Doug:** In that car going the other way.

**Norm:** Yeah!

**Doug:** Duck!

*They do. The streetcar fishtails wildly as it goes down the hill.*

**Norm:** Why'd he do it?

**Doug:** How'd I know? You got any ideas?

**Norm:** Well . . . no.

**Doug:** So shut up. I'm trying to think.

*Memory: the day of the picnic. Pete and Diane Thorpe enter the streetcar. Babe joins Doug and Norm.*

**Pete:** Y-you guys going to the picnic?

**Doug:** What do you think?

**Norm:** Yeah, whaddaya think?

*They look at Babe—he's distracted.*

**Doug:** What's with you today?

**Norm:** You smell funny.

**Babe:** Aftershave.

**Norm:** You shave?

**Babe:** Pipe down.

*The memory replays.*

**Doug:** What's with you today?

**Norm:** You smell funny.

**Babe:** Aftershave.

**Norm:** You shave?

**Babe:** Pipe down.

*And again:*

**Doug:** What's with you today?

**Norm:** You smell funny.

**Babe:** Aftershave.

**Norm:** You shave?

**Babe:** Pipe down.

*End of memory. The streetcar jerks to a stop. Everyone pours out but Norm and Doug.*

**Norm:** What are you thinking about?

**Doug:** Nothing.

**Norm:** Come on.

**Doug:** Let's get off here.

**Norm:** What are we gonna do?

**Doug:** How about we take in a flick?

**Chorus:** Now appearing at the Capital Theatre—Shirley Temple!

**Doug:** Nah!

*The boys react negatively.*

**Chorus:** Mae West at the Odeon!

**Norm:** No!

**Chorus:** Nell Gwyn at the Rialto!

**Doug:** Nope.

**Norm:** All soupy stuff.

**Doug:** Let's walk around. Look at stuff in windows.

**Chorus:** Uncle Ben's Hardware Store. Rope Sale.

*Something resembling Babe's corpse swings into view. The boys run.*

**Norm:** Let's go!

**Doug:** Cross 101 Street.

**Norm:** You mean jay-walk?

*Norm follows Doug across the street.*

**Various:** Downstairs in the Metropolitan department store, a lady was playing the piano.

After a thumping rendition of a Mozart minuet, someone requested a hymn.

**Chorus:** *Singing.* What a friend we have in Jesus . . .

*The boys run away.*

**Norm:** Every time you turn around!

**Doug:** Up the down escalator at Woodwards.

**Norm:** That floorwalker's following us—

**Doug:** He looks like Pete's dad.

**Norm:** Yeah!

**Chorus:** Frosted malts in the basement of the Bay.

**Doug:** You wanna go back over town? *Clive of India* is playing at the Princess.

**Norm:** My ma's going to pitch a fit if I miss supper.

**Doug:** It's not going to make any diff now. We're going to get it anyway.

**Norm:** I'll have to stay in for the rest of the summer.

**Doug:** Not a bad idea. We'd better stay on ice till the Cawners cool off. They'll want to know if Babe told us anything about the caves.

**Norm:** Geez, you don't think they think that we know what Babe knows?

**Doug:** Stop worrying.

**Norm:** Do you think they did something to Babe?

**Doug:** I don't know! Let's not talk about it, okay? *To audience.* At the Princess we sat through *Clive of India* one and a half times. I felt a lump in my throat as Ronald Coleman slowly put the pistol to his head.

*The boys slouch out of the theatre, at a loss about what to do next.*

**Doug:** Wanna sneak into the beer parlour at the Commercial Hotel?

**Norm:** No.

**Doug:** Wanna go back over town?

**Norm:** Nah, it's too late.

**Doug:** Let's go over to the train station. We could ride the rails.

**Norm:** Oh Dougie, I don't know . . .

**Doug:** Don't worry—I didn't mean it.

*A long, lonely-sounding train whistle. A long silence during which Norm finally starts to sniffle quietly. Doug struggles with himself, then finally follows suit. Babe appears in the background and seems to watch the boys.*

**Norm:** I don't understand . . . why . . . I don't understand . . .

**Doug:** Come on, Norm. It's okay.

**Norm:** It's not okay!

**Doug:** No, it's not.

**Norm:** What are we gonna do without Babe?

*The boys sit in silence.*

**Norm:** Why would he . . . do himself in?

**Doug:** He wouldn't.

**Norm:** Not Babe.

**Doug:** We gotta find out what happened to him.

**Norm:** Wh-what do you mean?

**Doug:** I mean we've gotta investigate.

**Norm:** Okay . . .

**Doug:** Come on. We can't sit here all night.

*Norm gets up, wipes his tears.*

**Doug:** We crossed the railway tracks . . . and started home.


## SCENE 9

*A crowd is gathered on the Roothes' front step, awaiting instructions from Albert to begin the search for the boys.*

**Albert:** A couple of you could have a look for the boys in the ravine.

**Mrs. Sayers:** Maybe we better wait for the police, Albert. The Cawners . . .

**Mr. Thorpe:** It wouldn't surprise me if the Cawners had something to do with all this.

**Albert:** That's enough.

**Mr. Thorpe:** They may have even influenced the young man—

**Albert:** I said that's enough. Now then, maybe you could go door to door.

*Mr. Sayers enters.*

**Mr. Sayers:** That won't be necessary, Albert. The boys have turned up.

*The neighbours start to disperse.*

**Albert:** I want to know why they ran away.

**Mr. Sayers:** Albert, you have all our sympathy, but the boys are tired.

**Albert:** I would like to speak to them—now.

**Mr. Sayers:** *After a beat.* Alright.

*Doug and Norm are ushered on to the porch just as a car door slam is heard offstage. Vic Bell enters.*

**Mr. Bell:** Albert . . . my deepest sympathies.

**Albert:** Thank you, Mr. Bell.

**Mr. Bell:** May I speak with you for a moment?

**Albert:** Certainly.

*Mr. Sayers makes a move to leave.*

**Albert:** If you don't mind, John, I'd still like to have a word with the boys.

*Mr. Sayers gestures to the boys to sit down again. Vic Bell and Albert enter the house.*

**Mrs. Sayers:** Who's that?

**Mr. Sayers:** It's Vic Bell, one of the Social Credit's city organizers.

**Mr. Bell:** Our prayers go with you, Albert.

**Albert:** Thank you, Vic. It's a terrible thing.

**Mr. Bell:** What happens now?

**Albert:** How do you mean?

**Mr. Bell:** Will there be an inquiry of some sort?

**Albert:** I expect so, yes. An inquest.

**Mr. Bell:** I see.

**Albert:** There may be a lot of publicity, Vic.

**Mr. Bell:** *With a nod.* The chief coroner is one of the UFA party faithful. I wouldn't be surprised if he tried to make some political hay out of this. You'll need to be strong.

*Albert nods.*

**Mr. Bell:** Listen, Albert—I can't help thinking of the lad Mr. Aberhart often mentions, who committed suicide because he couldn't take what economic conditions had done to his family.

*Albert seems to struggle with himself for a few moments before he replies.*

**Albert:** I don't think . . . we're not well-off, Vic, but I don't think that was the reason Babe . . .

**Mr. Bell:** I understand.

**Albert:** We won't be allowed to bury him till after the inquest so we're anxious to get it over with.

**Mr. Bell:** Yes. We all are. So your family can find some peace. *After a beat.* Once everything is settled . . . we had in mind you might consider running some meetings outside the city.

**Albert:** Of course I'll do it. Of course. *After a beat.* Probably good medicine. I must keep going.

**Mr. Bell:** Our deepest condolences once again. You will keep us advised, Albert, if there's anything we can do.

**Albert:** Yes sir, thank you sir.

*Vic Bell exits. Albert stares off into space.*

**Mr. Sayers:** I'm taking the boys home. We've all been through too much today. Albert?

*Albert doesn't respond.*

**Doug:** Albert. It was the first inkling I had that Babe's death was more than a tragedy. It was also an inconvenience.


## SCENE 10

*The Barker moves into position behind a podium/witness stand.*

**Barker**: Order! Order please!

**Doug:** The inquest. A complete waste of time. I know what Babe would have said.

**Babe:** What a bunch of clowns.

**Barker:** Order please! All rise for Dr. Candliss, Chief Coroner for the City of Edmonton. Members of the jury! You are instructed to determine for our Sovereign Lord the King the identity of the deceased, and when, where, and how and by what means the deceased . . .

*Doug and Norm sit in front of the witness stand.*

**Doug:** Babe . . .

**Barker:** . . . came to his death. For our Sovereign Lord the King.

**Doug:** Why. And why.

**Norm:** Geez the King wants to know?

**Barker:** Order! You may be seated.

**Coroner:** Albert Roothe.

**Albert:** The day after the picnic . . .

*Memory: Albert, Babe and Mrs. Roothe in the Roothe kitchen.*

**Albert:** Has Babe told you about his little disappearing act?

**Mrs. Roothe:** What do you mean?

**Albert:** Babe ditched Doug Sayers and the Fetterman boy as soon as they got to the rally.

**Babe:** We got separated.

**Mrs. Roothe:** There were a lot of people there.

**Albert:** Where'd you get to, Babe?

**Babe:** I was around.

**Albert:** I asked you a question. Where did you go?

**Babe:** Wouldn't you like to know?

**Albert:** Now listen, you. I have had enough of your—

**Mrs. Roothe:** Stop it both of you.

**Albert:** I've had enough—he can tell us, now—

**Mrs. Roothe:** Albert!

**Babe:** Do you want some help with the dishes, Mom?

**Mrs. Roothe:** I thought he wanted to talk to me about something. But he didn't.


## SCENE 11

*The Sayers household. Doug and Norm face a Policeman.*

**Police:** Why didn't you call on Babe Sunday?

**Doug:** I dunno. He ditched us at the fair so I guess we just thought we'd wait till he came around and told us all about it.

**Police:** You were mad at him?

**Doug:** I guess we were a bit peeved, yeah.

**Police:** You always do all the talking? You tell me, Norm. Why'd you boys go into the barn at that particular time? Come on.

**Norm:** We . . . we were trying to ditch this guy who was after us.

**Police:** Why was he after you?

**Norm:** We'd gotten too close to a place he didn't want us to be. That's all.

**Police:** Yeah? And who was this kid?

**Norm:** His name's Neil. Neil Cawner.

**Police:** A Cawner, eh? Well, well.

*The Policeman exits. Doug and Norm wander down the street.*

**Doug:** Everyone's interested in the Cawners aren't they?

**Norm:** What if they find out I told on them?

**Doug:** You never said nothing. It's old ratty Thorpe who was on about the Cawners.

**Norm:** What do you wanna do?

**Doug:** Dunno. I gotta think.

**Norm:** We could go swimming. Maybe your mom'll make us a sandwich.

**Doug:** I mean think about Babe.

**Norm:** Oh . . . yeah.

**Doug:** Maybe we could have another look in the barn.

**Norm:** Yeah!

**Doug:** Let's cut through Thorpes' yard.

*They hear Mr. Thorpe's roar just offstage. Doug pulls Norm into the sha-dows to watch Mr. Thorpe and Pete enter.*

**Mr. Thorpe:** Peter!

**Pete:** You promised! Y-you did!

**Mr. Thorpe:** I promised not to punish you for keeping the radio secret. I never said—

**Pete:** You c-can't take my radio!

**Mr. Thorpe:** Is that right?

**Pete:** It's not fair!

*Pete cowers for a moment. He knows he's gone too far. Mr. Thorpe grabs him tightly by the arm.*

**Mr. Thorpe:** What's fair? There's a heavenly judge of that, Peter. He judges all of us. He judges me. And He judges you.

*Mr. Thorpe gives Pete a shove and exits. Pete starts to slouch down the alley. Doug motions to Norm to follow him as they casually block Pete's way.*

**Doug:** Hey, Pete.

*Pete, suspicious about this overture, just looks at them.*

**Norm:** How are you, Pete?

**Pete:** Wh-what are you guys doin?

**Doug:** We're just asking around, that's all. About Babe. Your dad seemed to think the Cawners had something to do with it.

**Pete:** H-he . . . hates the Cawners.

**Doug:** I know—he was yelling about them the other night. Do you know why?

**Norm:** He know something about the Cawners?

**Doug:** Come on, Pete.

**Pete:** They're . . . s-sinners.

**Doug:** I coulda told you that. I'll tell you what I think. I think your dad ratted on the Cawners and they took it out on Babe. Does that sound right?

*Pete shakes his head and starts to back away.*

**Pete:** I gotta go.

**Doug:** Why don't you stay and shoot the breeze?

**Pete:** No.

**Norm:** Yeah. Let's shoot the breeze.

**Doug:** Or how about doing some Amos and Andy?

**Norm:** No, do the Shadow. Come on.

*Pete backs away, shaking his head.*

**Pete:** No. N-no more. I'm n-never going to—

**Doug:** Geez, Pete. Hope your dad doesn't take away your radio. We sure like all your radio voices.

*Pete stops dead, suddenly furious.*

**Pete:** No you don't. You don't!

*Pete runs away.*

**Doug:** That whole family's nuts.

**Norm:** Do you really think the Cawners killed Babe?

**Doug:** Dunno . . .

**Norm:** So now what?

**Doug:** Dunno. Why don't you come up with an idea for once?


## SCENE 12

**Chorus:** July 12.

**Various:** Another heat wave brought a shimmering unreality.

A red ball of sun dissolved the familiar shape of trees and houses into the wobbly outlines of mirage.

136 degrees in the sun on Thursday.

143 degrees on Friday.

The heat drove some of us down into our cellars . . .

. . . and the more fortunate ones to the Southside swimming pool.

There they jammed together in a steam of strong chlorine added to prevent infection among the thousands who used the place as an outhouse.

The Saturday paper came.

A reporter had fried some eggs on a manhole cover.

There would be a lunar eclipse on Monday night.

There was a brief report on Babe's inquest.

We let the heat flow over us and waited.


## SCENE 13

*The Inquest. Albert moves into the witness stand. Doug and Norm sit together and listen.*

**Coroner:** Now Mr. Roothe, I've been trying here to search out motive. What do you suppose put your brother in such a state that he wished to do away with himself?

**Albert:** I wish I knew.

**Coroner:** Now you're a religious and a political man, I believe.

**Albert:** Religious: yes. Political: no.

**Coroner:** Oh, I understand you are very active and well known in a certain political movement.

**Albert:** It's not political.

**Coroner:** I see. Did your brother belong to your . . . church?

**Albert:** No. I tried to get him interested in our youth groups. He came a couple of times, then quit.

**Coroner:** So he was not a religious boy? Would you say he was a sinner?

**Albert:** No more than any other boys his age.

**Coroner:** Did you invoke any visions of damnation or eternal fire when he wouldn't join your church group?

**Albert:** No, no. I wouldn't go that far.

**Coroner:** Not even for the Cause?

**Albert:** Of course not. I—I loved my brother.

**Doug:** *Whispering to Norm.* Yeah, sure.

**Coroner:** And yet you weren't close enough for him to confide his troubled state of mind?

**Albert:** Apparently not.

**Norm:** No kidding.

**Albert:** All I can say is . . . lately he had seemed . . . preoccupied.

**Norm:** What's preoccupied?

**Coroner:** About what? School, family . . . a girl?

**Albert:** *After a beat.* I don't know. He was a secretive boy. It was hard to know what was on his mind.

**Doug:** He's lying.

**Norm:** Do you think he'd lie?

**Coroner:** Boys! Shush, now.


**SCENE 14**

*Memory: Norm and Doug gather around Babe.*

**Babe:** Albert's after me again about his church group. He says if I join, I can go to a summer camp at Seba Beach.

**Doug:** Any dames?

**Babe:** I told you, the time I went to case the joint, all dogs.

**Doug:** What the hell, you'd be at the lake.

**Norm:** Yeah, why not?

**Babe:** He's just trying to get rid of me. You know, I think Jean likes me as much as she likes Albert.

**Norm:** *Appalled.* How old is she?

**Doug:** She's . . . beautiful.

**Babe:** She winked at me yesterday. Like we had a secret, the two of us.

**Doug**: Do you?

**Babe:** I winked back. Albert saw. Now he's going on about Bible camp. I told him I wasn't going and he got mad. Said "everything's so easy, isn't it"? And he slammed out of the house.

**Doug:** *Impressed*. He's . . . jealous!

**Babe:** *Shrugging it off*. Hey, I just don't wanna go to camp, okay. I've got other stuff to do.

*Pete enters, lurks nervously in the background.*

**Doug:** Where to?

**Babe:** Old Headley's barn.

**Norm:** It'll be pitch black in there.

**Babe:** *Shrugs*. Don't come then.

**Pete:** *Radio voice*. The Shadow knows.

**Norm:** How'd you do that?

**Pete:** I listen to the radio a lot.

**Babe:** Hey kid, what's your name?

**Pete:** Pete Thorpe. You guys goin' to that barn?

**Doug:** Maybe.

**Babe:** Where'd you move from anyway?

**Pete:** J-just over town.

**Babe:** Your dad get a new job?

**Pete:** N-no—we m-moved to a different church.

*Doug makes a face at Norm.*

**Babe:** You have a sister. What's her name?

**Pete:** *Imitating Diane.* My name is Diane Elizabeth Thorpe.

*Babe laughs appreciatively. Doug rolls his eyes.*

**Doug:** Are we going to the barn or not?

**Norm:** We won't be able to see a thing.

**Pete:** I—I got a candle. I'll go get it.

*Pete runs off.*

**Babe:** *Calling after him.* Good thinking, Pete. That way we can see what we're smoking.

*Pete returns, makes a gesture to the boys to hide inside the barn doors.*

**Pete:** *Imitating Mr. Thorpe.* Diane! Please come out here this instant. Diane!

*Diane emerges from the house, looks around, bewildered.*

**Diane:** Papa . . . ?

**Pete:** *As Mr. Thorpe.* Diane, come on out and meet the folks.

**Diane:** *Suspicious now.* Peter, is that you?

**Babe:** *From his hiding place.* Diane. Is that you?

*Norm and Doug are unable to contain themselves—they snicker.*

**Diane:** Very funny.

*Diane turns to go back in the house just as Mr. Thorpe arrives.*

**Mr. Thorpe:** Who are you talking to?

**Diane:** No one.

**Mr. Thorpe:** I heard you speaking to someone.

*Thorpe slowly approaches Diane, lays a hand on her shoulder. Diane looks uncomfortable.*

**Mr. Thorpe:** I can't believe you'd lie to me.

**Diane:** No, I wouldn't. I mean . . . I thought I heard you calling so I came outside.

**Mr. Thorpe:** And then . . .

**Diane:** *After a beat.* It was Peter. I was talking to Peter.

**Mr. Thorpe:** *Quickly pulling away from Diane and looking around the yard.* Where is he?

*Diane backs away, shaking her head, but her nervous glance toward the barn gives Pete away.*

**Mr. Thorpe:** Peter! Come out of that barn right now.

**Doug:** Geez, what's the big deal?

**Babe:** Let's get out of here!

*Babe and Norm scramble out, leaving Pete and Doug behind.*

**Mr. Thorpe:** I said now!

*Diane runs into the house, followed by Mr. Thorpe.*


## SCENE 15

**Coroner:** About four o'clock Sunday, Babe came upstairs and started reading a library book. The only unusual thing was his selection, a romance set in the court of King Charles the Second. When Mrs. Roothe went into his room, she noticed that the book was open and that Babe had pulled his chair over to the window where he was just staring out at the backyard. All he could have seen from there would have been the corner of Headley's barn and the garage in the yard next door. These neighbors are called Thorpe.

*Doug and Norm leave the inquest.*

**Doug:** Diane. Babe and Diane. They haven't even called her as a witness and she might have been one of the last ones to see him alive.

**Norm:** Sid Webb says it's all for show. The head guy thinks Babe did himself in—

**Doug:** What a dope! The whole thing's a big fat waste of time.

**Norm:** Yeah! A big fat waste—

*Mrs. Fetterman grabs Norm by the ear and hauls him away.*

**Mrs. Fetterman:** Come on, you! Jabbering in court—I was never so embarrassed!

**Norm:** Ow-ow-ow!

*Doug watches, then:*

**Doug:** When, where, and how did the deceased . . . no clues, Babe?

*Babe appears.*

**Babe:** Hey Dougie. Thought I better write you a note so you wouldn't worry. I'm taking off. It's too hot this summer and there's too many kids at Mill Creek Pool. I know a place where a guy can get a swimming hole all to himself. Just slip the old noose over your noggin, buddy. It won't hurt a bit . . .

**Doug:** *After a beat.* July 14. Taking matters into my own hands.

Almost midnight. The only sound is the clanking of the old mantel clock in the front room. I fiddle with the junk on my dresser and find the flashlight. Creep across the creaking floor and out into the night. Maybe Babe did the same thing, going to meet Diane. In the ravine? Nah. In the barn? Or maybe . . . I give in to pure inspiration.

I sneak into the Thorpes' garage.

**Chorus:** Dumb—stupid—get out before someone comes along.

**Doug:** The flashlight beam catches a splash of colour. It's a little piece of cloth with an embroidered edge, scrunched up and stuck together by something like a starch solution that had dried. I pick it up with shaky fingers, let myself out of the garage and run like hell.

## SCENE 16

*Doug's room. A knock on his door. He stuffs the hankie into his pocket as Norm enters.*

**Doug:** Hey, you're up early.

**Norm:** I came to say good-bye.

**Doug:** Where you going?

**Norm:** I'm going to visit my aunt in Calgary.

**Doug:** I thought you didn't like her. Isn't she real strict?

**Norm:** Yeah, but . . .

**Doug:** How long you going for?

**Norm:** For a few days, until things die down.

**Doug:** What?

**Norm:** *A tearful outburst.* Sid Webb says Joe Riley heard Billy Cawner wants to have a gab with you and me! The Cawners are after us, Dougie. They think we squealed on 'em!

**Doug:** Well we didn't, did we?

**Norm:** But the cops raided their place. They found all kinds of stolen stuff in the cave and they arrested Neil and Joe. They even killed one of their dogs—beaned him with a crowbar!

**Doug:** That's not our fault.

**Norm:** I'm scared!

**Doug:** It's okay! They can't do anything to us if they're in jail, right?

**Norm:** They won't be in jail forever.

**Doug:** So then we just spill the beans on old Thorpe—he's proably the one who turned them in. Now look—you can't go to Calgary.

**Norm:** I gotta. My mom needs to take in another boarder so we can pay our taxes. And besides—

**Doug:** Stop worrying about the Cawners. If you go, who's gonna help me investigate Babe?

**Norm:** There's nothing to investigate.

**Doug:** You're wrong about that. I'm going to show you something but you have to promise not to tell.

**Norm:** Is it something about the Cawners? Cause I don't wanna know anything—

**Doug:** Quit your blubbering, will you? I went into the Thorpes' garage last night and I found this.

*Doug reveals the hankie.*

**Norm**: What is it?

**Doug:** It belongs to Diane, I bet.

**Norm:** Big surprise. It was in her garage.

**Doug:** Well, look at it. What if Babe was there too?

**Norm:** What do you mean?

**Doug:** You don't get it, do you? She and Babe . . .

**Norm:** *After a beat, he doesn't get it.* Yeah, so what?

**Doug:** We're gonna ask her about it.

**Norm:** You can't. She's gone to some Bible school in Three Hills.

**Doug:** Three Hills? They sure packed her off in a hurry, didn't they?

**Norm:** Pete says Diane's going to go to school in Three Hills from now on.

**Doug:** You don't think that's funny?

**Norm:** I don't know, they were always holy rollers.

**Doug:** Come on, Norm. Think about it.

**Norm:** If it was important it woulda come up at the inquest.

**Doug:** They didn't know Babe. They didn't know about Babe and Diane. We didn't even know. I think they were meeting and we were too dumb to catch on.

**Norm:** Yeah. Maybe you're right. *Warming to the idea.* Then Diane gave him the brush-off and he couldn't stand it!

*Babe appears.*

**Babe:** *With heavy sarcasm.* Oh, darling. I can't bear to live without you.

**Doug:** Nah . . . sounds like a movie.

**Norm:** You got any better ideas?

**Doug:** I don't know. We'll go to Three Hills—we'll ask Diane.

**Norm:** Are you nuts?!

**Doug:** We'll . . . hitch-hike.

**Norm:** You are nuts.

**Doug:** We gotta do it. For Babe.

**Norm:** I don't know, Dougie.

**Doug:** Don't you think he'd do the same for us?

**Norm:** Mom says . . . she says it's not going to bring him back.

*Pause.*

**Doug:** *Bitterly.* No kidding.

**Norm:** I gotta go.

**Doug:** So go.

*Norm backs out of Doug's room with an apologetic look.*

## SCENE 17

**Coroner:** Gentlemen of the jury, harken to your verdict as record-ed by you. The date and time of death was July 7, 1935 at approximately midnight. The place of death was the loft of a barn at the rear of the property known as 9872-88 Ave. The cause of death was asphyxia due to hanging. The jury found this to be a most difficult case because of the apparently normal mental state of the deceased. However, on examining all the evidence, we un-animously agreed that we could offer no other verdict than that of suicide. So say you all?

**Jury Member:** Yes, sir.

**Coroner:** The inquest is now closed and the jury discharged. God save the King. All rise please.

*Babe appears, with another "suicide note."*

**Babe:** Dear Doug and Norm. *Beat.* Ally Oop.


## SCENE 18

**Mrs. Sayers:** July 16, 1935.

**Chorus:** The heat wave has broken.

**Barker:** For the first time since 1930 the price of wheat has bro-ken through the sixty-cent barrier. Throughout the region there are bumper crops coming into head. And for the first time in eight years . . .

**Child:** There's gonna be a parade!

**Various:** The Mammoth Prosperity Parade of 1935!
Crowds line Jasper Avenue
Two miles long!
Thirteen bands!
Forty floats!
One thousand marchers!

**Barker:** This year's gala grandstand presentation—

**Chorus:** Fascinations of 1935.

**Various:** Thrills, chills
The Royal American Midway
Thrill, chills
The Amazing Sky Rocket!

**Child:** Please!

**Adult:** Adults only!

**Mr. Sayers:** July 17, 1935.

**Albert:** Jean, Jean! The UFA's called the election for August 22nd!

**Jean:** That's wonderful!


## SCENE 19

*Doug runs out of his room and is about to leave the house when Mrs. Sayers stops him at the door.*

**Mrs. Sayers:** Where you off to?

**Doug:** Nowhere.

**Mrs. Sayers:** What's on your mind?

**Doug:** Nothing.

**Mrs. Sayers:** Dougie. What have you got hidden under your shirt?

*Doug slowly removes a bundle from under his shirt: a half loaf of bread.*

**Mrs. Sayers:** Okay, what's up?

**Doug:** I'm going on a little trip.

**Mrs. Sayers:** Is that right? By train? Bus? Private car?

**Doug:** I'm . . . going to hitchhike.

**Mrs. Sayers:** Do you know how hard that is, Doug? The roads are full of hobos and you're just a kid—

**Doug:** I'm going—you can't stop me!

**Mrs. Sayers:** Alright. I won't try. I imagine you can outrun me.

*Doug stops, confused.*

**Mrs. Sayers:** You expected more from the inquest, didn't you? More . . . answers.

**Doug:** And I'm going to get them.

**Mrs. Sayers:** The inquest was just meant to prove no crime was committed, that's all. It doesn't explain—

**Doug:** They never proved anything.

**Mrs. Sayers:** Maybe it would be easier to think Babe was the victim of some kind of plot—but he wasn't. He was obviously troubled about something—

**Doug:** He was not, he never was—

**Mrs. Sayers:** Doug . . . the Roothes buried Babe yesterday.

**Doug:** What do you mean? Why didn't they tell people?

**Mrs. Sayers:** They couldn't wait any longer. Albert . . . they all just wanted to get it over with. Why don't you visit Mrs. Roothe? I know she'd like to see you.

**Doug:** Albert! Albert couldn't wait!

*Doug slams out of the house. Mrs. Sayers watches him go.*


## SCENE 20

*The Roothe kitchen. Doug enters.*

**Doug:** Hello, Mrs. Roothe.

**Mrs. Roothe:** Dougie!

*She embraces Doug.*

**Mrs. Roothe:** Can I make you some lemonade? Sandwiches?

**Doug:** Sure, I guess.

**Mrs. Roothe:** I'm sorry we weren't able to let you know about the funeral, Dougie. We just weren't up to having the neighborhood there.

**Doug:** I understand.

*She hands a photo album to Doug.*

**Mrs. Roothe:** There's a lot of snapshots of you two. Why don't you have a look?

*As Doug looks, the snapshots become memories, elusive bits of Babe.*

**Babe:** I've got other stuff to do.

**Coroner:** The best and the brightest.

**Babe:** I've got other stuff to do.

**Coroner:** Hope. A careless slouching joy in life. Hope.

*Doug closes the album as Albert and Jean enter.*

**Albert:** Mom, they've asked me to do some speaking!

**Mrs. Roothe:** Hello, Jean.

**Albert:** It's quite an honour, really. They've got to be careful who they send into these rural areas. Feelings are running pretty high.

**Mrs. Roothe:** Where are you to go?

**Albert:** Three Hills.

*Doug nearly chokes on his sandwich.*

**Mrs. Roothe:** Dougie? Are you alright?

**Doug:** Mr. Aberhart is going to win the election, isn't he?

**Albert:** God grant us His blessing, yes. You interested in the election?

**Doug:** I hear a lot about it from my dad. He doesn't like Mr. Aberhart very much.

**Albert:** Well your father's in pretty tight with the socialists. Look

Doug, do you even know what socialism is?

*Doug shakes his head innocently.*

**Albert:** It'd mean that the government would run everything: all stores, movie houses, businesses, the whole works. You want a government to tell you how to do everything?

**Doug:** I don't know.

**Albert:** Well, holy mackerel, supposing that your entire life was run the way it is in school, with folks like teachers telling what you could do and when you could do it. Would you like that?

**Doug:** I guess not.

**Albert:** Okay, let's take it from another angle. What's the main thing people are short of these days?

**Doug:** Money—and I guess jobs.

**Albert:** Right. But jobs are created when there's enough money. Now supposing someone came up with a plan to create money, without having to bring in a system of socialism?

**Doug:** Sounds okay. But where'd they get the money from?

**Albert:** Aha, you've hit the nub of the whole issue, this entire campaign, this struggle for hearts and minds.

**Jean:** And souls. Don't forget the souls.

**Albert:** Social Credit is a scientific method of providing the people with the purchasing power to be free again. Would you like to know more about it?

**Doug:** I sure would.

**Mrs. Roothe:** Why don't you take young Doug with you to Three Hills? He could see a meeting and actually hear you speak.

*Jean makes frantic "no" signals behind Mrs. Roothe's back.*

**Albert:** I don't know.

**Mrs. Roothe:** All the neighborhood boys seem to be off at camps and things. It would be nice for Dougie to have a little trip.

**Doug:** I'd sure love to go.

**Albert:** Well, if it's alright with your dad, Doug . . .

**Doug:** Oh, I'm sure he won't mind.

**Albert:** Fine. We should make an early start.


## SCENE 21

*The Three Hills rally. Crowd noise as Albert ascends the grandstand.*

**Albert:** *Nervous.* Good evening. Uh . . . good evening, ladies and gentlemen . . .

*The crowd is restless, but mostly attentive now, except for few whispers and murmurs.*

**Albert:** Thank you. Mr. Aberhart has asked me to speak to you about the new economic policies proposed by—

**Heckler:** Liars!

**Albert:** Proposed by . . . Mr. Aberhart. *A beat to collect himself.* We have studied the economic situation long and hard, and we have prayed—

**Heckler:** Liars! Holy rollers!

**Albert:** Social Credit is a system of creating—

**Heckler:** Creating votes!

*Crowd noise increases.*

**Albert:** Listen to me! I know you're angry. You think I don't know about your misery? You have seen the banks turn the bounty given to you by God into worthless paper. You're selling your livestock at a loss because you can't afford to feed them. Some of you have even lost your farms. All this . . . when the only thing you want . . . is to feed your families.

*A respectful silence, except for:*

**Heckler:** *Grumbling to himself.*

**Albert:** Sir? Now I don't have any objections if you want to come up here and state what your party, whichever one it is, will do to relieve the pain.

**Heckler:** Liberal!

**Supporter:** Oh, go home!

**Albert:** It seems to me, though, that all of you old-line parties have had your chance and yes, I include the Communists and the Socialists, too, for nothing could be older than the slavery they preach. I'd say—it's time for a change.

*Clapping and cheering from the crowd.*

**Albert:** Please join me in singing . . .

**Doug:** I snuck out of the rally and headed for the Bible school.

*A rousing version of "What a Friend We Have in Jesus." Albert begins to move through the crowd, shaking hands, etc.*

**Chorus:** *Singing.* What a friend we have in Jesus,
All our sins and griefs to bear!
What a privilege to carry
Everything to God in prayer!
Oh what peace we often forfeit,
Oh what needless pain we bear,
All because we do not carry
Everything to God in prayer.


## SCENE 22

*The crowd begins to move out of town meeting configuration and into the Bible school promenade. Bibles clasped to their chests, one or two of them still hum "What A Friend We Have in Jesus." Doug enters the yard.*

**Doug:** I crept to the edge of the school yard and watched the girls promenade, Bibles clasped to their chests.

Hi, Diane. It's me, Doug.

*A hissing begins in the girls' group.*

**Various:** Di, Di—who is he?
    The rules—tell him to go.
    Hey, you, you're not allowed here.
    Scram.
    Beat it.

**Doug:** I gotta talk to you.

*Chorus repeats "scram" and "beat it" under the following.*

**Diane:** You better leave.

**Doug:** I just happened to be in the neighborhood. Thought I'd say hello.

**Diane:** What do you want?

**Doug:** I wanna talk about Babe.

**Diane:** I don't know anything—

**Doug:** I know he was sweet on you—

**Diane:** I never said anything to him!

**Doug:** *Holding out an envelope containing the hankie.* Here, take this, it's yours. Babe wanted you to have it.

*Diane opens the envelope.*

**Doug:** Come on, Diane. You know, don't you?

**Diane:** Where did you get this?

**Doug:** I found it in your garage.

**Diane:** Get out of here.

*A school official appears at the edge of the yard.*

**Doug:** Diane, please! Maybe you had nothing to do with it. But you saw him just before—you talked to him. Please, I gotta know. Why would Babe kill himself?

**Diane:** He wouldn't—he wouldn't!

**Doug:** What do you mean? What happened?

**Diane:** Go away!

*The volume of the Chorus reaches a climax as Diane runs away. Doug tries to follow—he's confronted by a school official.*

**Official:** You don't belong here, son. Please go.

**Doug:** I gotta see her.

**Official:** Well she doesn't want to see you. You'd better go.


## SCENE 23

*The Chorus comes forward and closes in on Doug with the following.*

**Various:** July 22, 1935.
    Ten inches of rain north of Calgary.
    A border collie in Fort Saskatchewan survives a hit of lightning.
    A farmhouse in the path of a brush fire burns, killing three children.
    Smoke darkens the skies above Edmonton.

**Doug:** Babe . . .

**Mrs. Sayers:** A perfectly healthy boy.

**Mrs. Roothe:** He was a happy boy. Wasn't he?

**Albert:** Secretive.

**Jean:** Senseless. So young.

**Norm:** What are we gonna do without Babe?

**Doug:** No note, no message, no clue.

*The Chorus recedes a little as Babe creeps out of the shadows. He and Doug share a look.*

**Doug:** Babe—I'm not giving up.

*Blackout. End of Act One.*

**On the streetcar on the way to the Northern Alberta Social Credit Picnic.**
playRites '99, Calgary.

**Social Credit Political Meeting.**
playRites '99, Calgary.

**Allan Morgan as Mr. Thorpe, Tara Hughes as Diane Thorpe.**
playRites '99, Calgary.

**Brian Marler as Peter Thorpe, Kevin Kruchkywich as Doug Sayers.**
playRites '99, Calgary.

# ACT TWO

**SCENE 24**

*A banner is erected, proclaiming "German-Canadian Picnic."*

**Doug:** Sunday, August 4, 1935.

**Barker:** Southside Athletic Grounds.

The Eighth Annual Picnic of the German-Canadian Reunion Association.

**Doug:** I went because I had nothing better to do. The German-Canadians were eager to hear about the economic miracle in their homeland. And the local politicians were desperate to capitalize on the good news from abroad. Including Albert.

**Barker:** Speeches, musical entertainment, prizes and fun for the whole family! Potato races—hundred-yard dash, seventy-five for women—high jump and . . .

Tug-of-war.

City versus country.

**Doug:** All this cheerful nationalism seemed innocent enough until a few years later when I was staring down the barrel of a German gun. The war took its toll on our little neighborhood.

*Carnival atmosphere in full swing. People mill about the grandstand, eating hot-dogs, running races, etc. As the Union Jack is raised, the crowd sings the first line of "God Save the King." As the German flag is raised, the crowd sings the first line of "Deutschland Uber Alles." The speakers ascend the grandstand, including Albert. Doug takes up a perch underneath.*

**Barker:** Herr Doctor Seelheim, German Consul-General for western Canada.

**Seelheim:** Rebuilding Germany . . . National Socialism. We are winning the battle against the excesses of capitalism. Jobs—food on every table—security for all good Germans. Rejuvenation . . . revitalization . . . a new world order.

*Seelheim's speech is greeted with cheers.*

**Barker:** Mr. Lymburn, Attorney General for the United Farmers of Alberta.

**Lymburn:** Hard working, conscientious, dedicated. These hallmarks of the German ethnic tradition, qualities which we will be in desperate need of as we begin the difficult task of rebuilding the province.

*Polite applause.*

**Barker:** Mr. Duggan, leader of the provincial Conservative Party.

**Duggan:** I appeal to all German-Canadians . . . join with us to preserve, during the present times of unrest, that which has been built by the pioneers . . .

*Polite applause.*

**Barker:** Mr. Howson, leader of the Liberal Party of Alberta.

**Howson:** Honour the older people who came to this land to give their children greater opportunity. I urge you younger ones . . . carry on in the same pioneering spirit.

*Polite applause.*

**Barker:** Mr. Albert Roothe, speaking on behalf of the Social Credit Party.

**Albert:** I bring you greetings from our leader, Mr. Aberhart, who, as you know, is of German ancestry himself. I know he would have wanted to be here. Doctor Seelheim has very graphically described the new winds of change that are sweeping Germany today. A similar urge for change now grips the people of Alberta. We, too, stand at the crossroads, where we must decide to continue as we have been doing these past few years or seek a new way, a new order. In this sense we are all pioneers again. Thank you.

*Enthusiastic applause. The crowd begins to reprise "Deutschland Uber Alles" as they raise their arms in a Nazi salute, one by one. Finally everyone has an arm raised in a Nazi salute except Albert. He raises his arm, then changes his mind at the last moment, and places his hat on his heart. Doug catches Albert's eye—they stare at each other.*

**Doug:** Atta boy, Albert!

*Albert frowns. Doug turns to the audience.*

**Doug:** Someone had to pick up where Babe had left off, undermining Albert's sweaty earnestness with cool sass. I tried to imagine what Babe would have done, if he'd been here, watching Albert's transformation into a smooth politician. And in doing so I began to realize what a threat Babe posed to Albert's self-confidence. Babe would have been here alright, pure anarchy at the age of fifteen, to mock Albert's progress and remind him that their mother still made his lunch.

## SCENE 25

*The Chorus moves into place, newspapers in hand.*

**Mrs. Fetterman:** August 6—the day the storms came.

**Various:** The elements went wild.
The faint haze of rain was swept aside by a solid wall of hail,
pounding in slanted waves of rolled ice
that bounced and clattered off the ground and steps.
The garden disappeared under jiggling piles of hail,
like a plague of bluish-white frozen termites.

**Mrs. Sayers:** My God, did you see that? That's the end of the garden.

**Mr. Sayers:** And every poor bastard of a farmer.

**Norm:** Chickens were pulverized until they were only bloody clumps of feathers.

**Mrs. Fetterman:** Cows and horses went crazy in the slashing torrents.

**Various:** East of Calgary the hail lay over a foot thick on the ground.

After it melted they found partridges and pheasants beaten to death, their wings stretched over their dead young.

Hailstones the size of eggs wrecked the nearly perfect crops.

**Mrs. Fetterman:** Eggs? My sister's neighbour was knocked out cold by a stone the size of a pumpkin.

**Norm:** Mom!

**Mrs. Fetterman:** It's true! My sister says it couldn't have happened to a better person.

**Mr. Thorpe:** Mrs. Fetterman!

**Mrs. Sayers:** Again and again the massive blue thunderheads piled up in grinning skulls, picked the targets they had missed, then struck.

**Mr. Sayers:** The force of nature.

**Mr. Thorpe:** What is the force of nature but the wrath of God?


## SCENE 26

*The Sayers household. Doug enters doing a Hitler imitation, complete with a black-comb mustache, goose-stepping. Mrs. Sayers follows him into their house.*

**Doug:** *Bad German accent.* Ve vill make sausages!

**Mrs. Sayers:** *Laughing in spite of herself.* Dougie, that's terrible.

**Doug:** Zeig heil!

*Mr. Sayers enters just as Doug does the Nazi salute.*

**Mr. Sayers:** Do you know what you're doing?

**Mrs. Sayers:** Oh, John, he was just kidding around.

**Mr. Sayers:** Well stop it. Look at this. *Reading from newspaper.* Near Frienwalde, Germany, a notice was posted reading, "the smell of Jew is deadly in the pure forest air." Municipal officials have been ordered to cease all business and social intercourse with Jews. That little man is no Charlie Chaplin. And Albert and his bunch aren't that much different. All their talk of Zionist plots.

**Mrs. Sayers:** But not Albert . . .

**Mr. Sayers:** You heard what Dougie told us about the rally, how Albert toadied up to them. They're dangerous!

**Mrs. Sayers:** John . . .

**Mr. Sayers:** They interrupted our meeting tonight. A few bully boys let some air out of tires and painted Social Credit on car hoods. They were yelling about the evils of socialism just outside the window until it got so disruptive we had to stop.

**Mrs. Sayers:** Surely you're not saying they're as bad as this Hitler?

**Mr. Sayers:** I think they're just as fanatical. Everybody's been whipped up into such a state, with the poverty and the politics. There's a kind of frenzy in the air. And if you want my opinion it's all the worse that it's disguised as religion.

*Mr. Thorpe bursts into the Sayers house, waving a letter.*

**Mr. Thorpe:** You! You molested my daughter! You had the nerve to—to—

**Mr. Sayers:** Now, now, Mr. Thorpe. What's all this?

**Mr. Thorpe:** Your son went all the way to the Institute to assault my daughter. She wrote me about it—

**Mr. Sayers:** Wait a minute. This true, Doug?

**Doug:** I just thought I'd go and see how she was . . .

**Mr. Sayers:** Mr. Thorpe, what did Diane actually say?

*Mr. Thorpe reluctantly gives the letter to Sayers as Diane appears in the shadows.*

**Diane:** We had a revelation the other day. Tom, who comes from Stettler, came forward to the Mercy Seat to confess his sins aloud. We all got caught up in it and began to shout out our own confessions. I'd never seen anything like it, Papa. Wish you could have seen it too. Meant to tell you, I had a visit last Saturday from one of the neighbors. It was Doug Sayers. I didn't want to see him so they sent him away. Hope he never comes back.

*Diane withdraws.*

**Mr. Sayers:** All right, the boy shouldn't have done that.

**Mr. Thorpe:** I want to know what he was doing—

**Mr. Sayers:** That's for me to find out. I'll talk to the boy and I'll thank you not to bother him again about it. We're sorry.

**Mr. Thorpe:** That's all you have to say? Here he goes into a place of Christian study to disturb a poor girl who is trying to find her way to the Truth, and you—

**Mr. Sayers:** Enough, Mr. Thorpe. That's it.

*Mr. Thorpe storms off.*

**Doug:** He's nuts.

**Mr. Sayers:** Doug . . .

**Mrs. Sayers:** I think his job's getting to him.

**Mr. Sayers:** At least he has one.

**Mrs. Sayers:** Exactly. Think of the power he wields over people's lives with his tax assessments. He feels guilty. A lot of city folks were counting on tax money from some country cousin with a good crop and now . . . after all that hail.

**Mr. Sayers:** Now Mr. Thorpe will have to wait until they get their twenty-five dollars a month.

*Mr. Sayers nods significantly toward Doug.*

**Mrs. Sayers:** You wanna tell your dad about your trip to the Bible Institute, Doug?

*Mrs. Sayers exits.*

**Mr. Sayers**: I think I know why you went to see Diane. You wanna talk about it?

**Doug:** I found this hankie, I'm sure it was hers. I think she and Babe were together before he . . . before he died.

**Mr. Sayers:** Doug, in a court of law that would be circumstantial evidence at best. You know what that means? Unless there was some kind of corroborating statement, it wouldn't prove anything about Babe's death.

**Doug:** If she would admit they were together, it would prove something.

**Mr. Sayers:** You think Babe killed himself over a girl?

**Doug:** Naw, not Babe.

**Mr. Sayers:** Then what would it prove to hear from Diane?

**Doug:** I think she's hiding something. She talked to him right before it happened. She knew what he was thinking.

**Mr. Sayers:** There was an inquest, Dougie. They never found any evidence.

**Doug:** They never even called her as a witness. Or the Cawners.

**Mr. Sayers:** What about the Cawners?

**Doug:** He hung around with them for a bit. Maybe he knew too much about what was in their cave. After he beat up Billy Cawner they were pals, see?

**Mr. Sayers:** You've been thinking about this a lot, haven't you?

**Doug:** Someone has to! Everyone else just let it go, even the people who should care most. Like Albert. Why doesn't he want to know what happened to Babe?

**Mr. Sayers:** Albert has other things on his mind these days.

**Doug:** Sometimes when I go to see Mrs. Roothe—she brings out the photo albums and we talk about Babe. If Albert's there, he always leaves the room, like it makes him mad or something.

**Mr. Sayers:** Dougie, Dougie, settle down. Did you ever think that he might just be trying to forget? And what about Diane? If she did have something to do with Babe killing himself, what kind of pain do you think you caused her by bringing it up again?

**Doug:** I don't know. But that still doesn't—

**Mr. Sayers:** Okay, listen. Did you ever think about the possibility of it being an accident?

**Doug:** How do you mean?

**Mr. Sayers:** I mean, maybe Babe was fooling around, showing off—and things got out of hand.

*Babe appears in the barn, playing with the noose.*

**Babe:** Hey, Dougie. If you had to pick how you were gonna go . . . Arsenic? A bullet to the brain?

**Doug:** So who was he showing off to?

**Mr. Sayers:** Maybe Diane. Maybe no one. Maybe he was practicing a trick to show you boys another time.

**Babe:** Slip a little rope around your neck.

**Mr. Sayers:** You boys played in the barn all the time, didn't you?

**Doug:** Yeah . . .

**Babe:** They say your whole life flashes in front of your eyes.

**Mr. Sayers:** Maybe he was playing and . . . he just went too far.

*Doug stares off, considering this.*

**Mr. Sayers:** Everyone's just trying to forget, Dougie. Maybe you should do the same.

*Mr. Sayers exits, leaving Doug deep in thought.*

## SCENE 27

*Inquest.*

**Coroner:** What you're saying is you can't surmise a motive for your friend to . . . do away with himself?

**Doug:** That's right, sir.

**Coroner:** Now consider this. Do you feel it's possible he might have been in love with death itself? Alright, take your time.

**Doug:** No, sir. I don't really know what you mean, but I can't believe anyone'd have that kind of feeling. Unless he was nuts.

**Coroner:** It has been known as a condition of the human soul.

**Doug:** No, sir. Babe wasn't like that. He wasn't insane.

*The Coroner melts away.*

**Doug:** I never thought Babe was crazy. He was better, brighter than the rest of us, with his big ideas and wild streaks. Taunting the Cawners. Walking along the railway tracks on top of the High Level Bridge. Riding his bike at breakneck speed down Walterdale Hill, then suddenly putting his hands behind his head. It was a kind of craziness, I spose. *Beat.* Or maybe I was the crazy one, still poking through the ashes. Going over the possibilities. Even though sometimes I could barely remember his face.

## SCENE 28

*Albert and Jean sit on the porch, necking. Doug wanders up, then hides.*

**Albert:** There are so many who are worthy to run as candidates, Jean. I could easily be passed over.

**Jean:** Vic Bell practically promised you.

**Albert:** Did you ask your dad about borrowing the car again?

**Jean:** He said fine. But this time he wants a guarantee about his twenty-five dollars a month.

**Albert:** Your dad's quite a kidder.

**Jean:** He wasn't kidding. Come 'ere.

*Jean kisses Albert passionately. Albert breaks away.*

**Albert:** I just can't help thinking . . .

**Jean:** Me neither—

**Albert:** There's Doctor Willis—he's been with the movement since the start. There's Orvis Kennedy—he's been very active with youth groups.

**Jean:** But he can't speak as well as you. You're young, you know the policies backwards and forwards. You . . . are the best man for the job.

**Doug:** *Blurting it out.* Albert feels guilty, huh? About Babe?

**Jean:** What are you talking about?

**Doug:** What's he feel guilty about?

**Jean:** Forget it, Doug. And no more sneaking up on people, okay?

*Jean moves off. Just before she exits—*

**Jean:** August 7th. Aberhart announces his Edmonton slate.


## SCENE 29

*The Roothe household. Mrs. Roothe sets sandwiches in front of Doug. Albert scans the paper.*

**Mrs. Roothe:** Who have they chosen, Albert?

**Albert:** All fine men. Not surprised about Dr. Hall, after all he's chairman of City Central. A dentist, you've met him, Mom: glasses, wavy hair. Your dad must know Dr. Willis, Doug; he was a high-school teacher at Vic, now he's vocational head over at the Board. Good man. Gil King is one of our best organizers, but in all charity, I'd say I've done as much.

**Mrs. Roothe:** Don't feel too badly. They must have some plans for you.

**Albert:** I wonder, Mom. More speeches? Mr. Aberhart says he's trying to free the Movement from the old-line politicians, but then he goes on to say many of the candidates named ran for other parties in previous elections. I don't know why he did that when there are so many of us who aren't connected with the old-line parties in any way.

**Mrs. Roothe:** Come on Albert, he's a smart politician.

**Albert:** That's not so, Mom. Mr. Aberhart isn't even running for a seat. If the people want him after the election, a place will be found for him.

**Doug:** My dad says that's the world's oldest boondoggle.

**Albert:** Well your dad is going to get a surprise on election day, Doug.

**Doug:** Oh he won't be surprised, he'll just be disgusted.

*Albert considers Doug for a moment.*

**Albert:** You still interested in politics, Doug? Or do you just like to hear me speak?

**Doug:** Both, I guess.

**Albert:** I could have sworn you came to Three Hills so you could bother the Thorpe girl.

**Mrs. Roothe:** What's this?

**Albert:** Dougie had a little run-in at the Bible Institute.

**Doug:** I tried to talk to Diane.

**Mrs. Roothe:** Well that's natural, isn't it? An old school friend.

**Doug:** She and Babe were sweet on each other. I just wanted to talk to her, to ask her—

**Albert:** That's enough!

**Mrs. Roothe:** It's alright, Albert. It's alright.

**Albert:** That's why you wangled an invitation to Three Hills, isn't it?

**Doug:** No, I wanted to hear you . . . carry the word.

*Doug and Albert stare at one another, long and hard.*

**Albert:** If that's the case, I'm sure you and your friends will want to help out at the polls on election day. I'll let them know at central office.

**Mrs. Roothe:** Babe was . . . interested in the Thorpe girl? I never knew that. Did you know that, Albert?

**Doug:** Yeah, he knew that.

*Albert shoots Doug a furious look.*

**Albert:** I'm going to see if Jean can get the car tonight. We'll go to the rally over at the Franciscan Hall and see how our new and wonderful slate handles itself.

*Babe appears out of the shadows and grins at Albert.*

**Babe:** Maybe next time.


## SCENE 30

*Doug pokes along the sidewalk, deep in thought. Norm enters at a run.*

**Norm:** Dougie! I'm back!

**Doug:** Hi.

**Norm:** Well geez—are you glad to see me or what?

**Doug:** Of course I am. How was Calgary?

**Norm:** I nearly starved to death at my aunt's. But I saw some cowboys!

**Doug:** No kidding.

**Norm:** What's up, anyway? You look like someone died.

*Doug looks at Norm like he's crazy.*

**Norm:** You're not still . . . ?

**Doug:** What else have I got to do? I'm practically the only guy left in the neighborhood. You left; Sid Webb's got a new gang over town.

**Norm:** And Billy Cawner's gone to reform school! Our troubles are over!

**Doug:** Yeah, sure . . .

**Norm:** So . . . you figure anything out?

**Doug:** Just . . . I think Albert knows more than he's saying. I think he knew about Diane—but I can't prove it.

**Norm:** Holy moly—do you think Albert killed Babe?

*Doug shoots Norm a disgusted look.*

**Doug:** No, I don't think that. Geez, Norm.

**Norm:** What?

**Doug:** You're such a baby.

**Norm:** What? What's wrong with you? Dougie!

*Doug just shakes his head and walks away from Norm who shuffles off, disappointed. Doug turns back, as if observing his younger self.*

**Doug:** Dougie . . .

*Doug shakes off the moment.*


**SCENE 31**

**Doug:** August 10.

*Albert runs on.*

**Albert:** Jean! Jean, come quickly!

*Jean appears, wearing a housecoat.*

**Albert:** Sorry to wake you but Jean—they want me to go to Calgary for an interview at Mr. Aberhart's Prophetic Bible Institute.

**Jean:** That's wonderful! What does it mean, do you think?

**Albert:** I'm not going to jump to any conclusions until I talk to them. Maybe they want me to work as a campaign manager.

**Jean:** Or maybe this time . . .

*Albert runs off. Jean watches him go.*

**Doug:** Albert was so excited he nearly drove Jean's father's car off the road on the way to Calgary. Albert wouldn't have gone out of his way to tell me that. But I got the lowdown from Jean years later. *Exchanges a look with Jean, who smiles, pulls her house-coat around her and exits.* In London, during the war—Jean and I shared a bed and a bottle of gin. But that's another story.

## SCENE 32

*Two Social Credit Examiners and Aberhart take their seats opposite Albert. They laugh together as Albert turns to face them.*

**Examiner #1:** I can see why you're in demand as a speaker!

**Aberhart:** Oh, is he?

**Examiner #2:** Indeed, he is. We've been using Mr. Roothe at quite a few places.

**Examiner #1:** Suppose we are successful in putting Social Credit in here. What then?

**Albert:** I'll be frank with you: sometimes I despair at the forces lined up against us, but when Mr. Aberhart speaks, my faith is refreshed again.

**Aberhart:** What are these forces that cause you such despair?

**Albert:** As I see it, it goes much deeper than the misguided, tin-horn politicians who oppose Social Credit. Or even the Fifty Bigshots. There are more sinister powers arrayed against us. They control the banking system, international finance, the press, political parties, legislatures, and parliaments.

**Examiner #2:** Go on.

**Albert:** Well, gosh, you take the guys who control Wall Street, they're of the same Turko-Mongolian stock as the Communists and the Free Masons. And they're all tied in with the Zionists. They're against everything that is white, Anglo-Saxon—especially the British Empire. I can't help but think of what Ernest Manning said in that speech he gave at King Edward Hall. Not only do we have to contend with non-Christian forces—we are up against a non-Christian conspiracy.

**Examiner #1:** Against such forces, what can we do here?

**Albert:** We must win the next election so that we will have the foundation, the rock against which these alien forces will destroy themselves.

*A respectful silence.*

**Examiner #2:** Thank you, Albert.

**Aberhart:** Albert, we've been hearing fine reports on your work. I'm told you wowed them at the German rally. Good stuff.

**Albert:** Thank you, Mr. Aberhart.

**Aberhart:** You are aware that nominations close at two o'clock tomorrow?

**Albert:** Yes sir.

**Aberhart:** Are you knowledgeable at all about the constituency of Strathcona-Whitemud?

**Albert:** Yes, I've given three speeches there. The candidate, Fred Tarrow, is a fine man. He shouldn't have any trouble getting elected.

**Aberhart:** Then you haven't heard what happened to him?

**Albert:** No.

**Aberhart:** Late Friday night, driving home from a meeting, Fred had an accident. He has a concussion and several broken bones.

**Albert:** I'm sorry to hear that.

**Aberhart:** Well chances are he could get elected from his hospital bed. Except for one minor but important fact about his accident. He was obviously driving much too fast for his fatigued state and . . . the police report says he had been drinking. Frankly, Albert, we can't afford to have any of our members elected under a cloud of that nature. We have gone to the voters saying we are honest, clean, Christian, a new wave of dedicated politicians who won't be corrupted or side-tracked from our duty to the public. Mr. Gould has been to see Mr. Tarrow and has obtained his resignation. Hence—and I won't beat around the bush any longer—your name has come up.

**Albert:** I see.

**Aberhart:** We want you to accept the nomination. If you wish to take a while to pray and meditate in the chapel—

**Albert:** No, no, it's alright. I'd be honoured to accept.

**Aberhart:** Fine, fine. Very good.

**Albert:** Now I think I would like to retire to your chapel, if I may.

**Aberhart:** By all means.

**Albert:** Well thank you, all of you. I hope you'll pray for me.

**Aberhart:** We shall. We shall indeed, Albert.

*Albert wanders off in a trance.*

**Chorus:** Atta boy, Albert!


## SCENE 33

**Mr. Sayers:** *Angrily slapping his newspaper shut.* They're going to make it, the whole damned lot of them.

**Doug:** Albert's going to win?

**Mrs. Sayers:** Is it really so bad, John?

**Mr. Sayers:** It's just—they're so sanctimonious, so sure of their economic rubbish. You know they won't be able to put it in, and I suspect they know it too. That's what's wrong.

*Chorus trickles in.*

**Various:** *Overlapping.* How do you know they won't?
How do you know, eh?
Least we can do is give them a chance.

What we need is a big change.
Why don't you just shut up and see what they can do?
Someone completely different/a big change.
You got yer monetization/of credit,
Twenty-five dollars/a month.
Fifty big-shots./This country needs a big change!
Thursday, August 15.
Aberhart at the Oliver School.

**Aberhart:** Out with the old-line parties!

**Albert:** Aberhart speaks to the Economic Safety League.

**Aberhart:** Your president is nothing but a super-heterodyne Liberal!

**Albert:** The Alberta Avenue Community Hall.

**Aberhart:** You don't have to know all about Social Credit theory before you vote for it. You don't have to understand electricity to make use of it.

**Albert:** Westmount Community Hall.

**Aberhart:** Look me straight in the eye. Do I look as if I'm trying to pull something over on you? I only want to put in monetary policies which could deliver your twenty-five dollars a month. In fact, if all goes well . . . the dividend could be as much as seventy-five dollars a month.

**Heckler:** You're crazy!


**SCENE 34**

**Mrs. Sayers:** August 16th.

**Mrs. Roothe:** Frost–
A last low blow from the elements.
White-coated blades of grass crackled and snapped off underfoot.

**Mrs. Sayers:** Rows of potatoes, beans, and peas,
   their leaves already tattered from the hail,
   partially buried where they had been pounded into the soil by
   the heavy rains.

**Mr. Sayers:** Even the dahlias are edged in white.

**Mrs. Fetterman:** That's it for the gardens. And the last of the
   crops.

**Mr. Sayers:** There's nothing left for them now.

**Various:** Mr. Thorpe, apparently gone mad,
   Stomped up and down the alley by the gardens,
   Picking up rotten vegetables and shaking them at the heavens,
   As if he'd be happy to have the guilty party step outside for a
   punch.


## SCENE 35

**Doug:** Frost on my bedroom window. A design of tiny jagged
   stars. I stared at the pane of glass. Something was trying to
   edge into my consciousness, but it kept slipping out of reach.
   Jack Frost takes every breath you breathe. And knows the
   things you think about. Those stars on the window were trying
   to tell me something.

*Memory: Mrs. Roothe on the stand at the inquest.*

**Mrs. Roothe:** I went into Babe's room to do some dusting and I
   noticed that he had pulled his chair over to the window where
   he was just staring out at the backyard. All he could see from
   there would have been our backyard, my vegetable garden and
   some of the Thorpe's yard next door. And . . . the edge of the
   barn . . . where he . . . it's two lots away.

**Doug:** I padded over to my window and stared out at the brilliant
   moonlit stillness and felt the slight breeze, clammy on my

sweaty pajamas. I pushed up the sill of the inner glass window. I unhooked the screen and tried to jiggle it around and take it off from the inside. There was a groove that held it in place and the four outer tabs made it impossible to move. Just like Babe's window. Someone else must have been outside to move the tabs into a vertical position so the screen could be lifted off.

Someone had called on him that night!

## SCENE 36

*The Roothe household. Mrs. Roothe pours lemonade for Doug, who is extremely restless.*

**Mrs. Roothe:** You looking forward to going back to school?

**Doug:** Not really.

**Mrs. Roothe:** Young Norm back from Calgary yet?

**Doug:** Yes, ma'am.

**Mrs. Roothe:** Dougie . . . ?

**Doug:** Would it be alright if I looked in Babe's room for a minute?

**Mrs. Roothe:** I guess—

*Albert enters.*

**Mrs. Roothe:** Albert! For heaven's sake—we didn't know if we'd see you for another week.

**Albert:** We've been out in those shanty towns south of the city where the water mains end. It's muddy, let me tell you.

**Mrs. Roothe:** What a nice surprise to see you.

**Albert:** Thought I'd better get another change of clothes.

**Mrs. Roothe:** You look tired.

**Albert:** I feel . . . tremendous. It's going very well.

**Mrs. Roothe:** Mr. Headley told us he saw you the other day when he was on his rounds filling water cans. He said you looked very authentic.

**Albert:** He said that?

**Mrs. Roothe:** Actually he said, "Nothing like rubber boots to give you the clodhopper look. Albert looked as if he'd been busting sod all his life."

**Albert:** Yes, ma'am. We are gettin' a mighty fine reception from the folks. In an ordinary campaign it'd be nuts to go in at the last minute the way I have, but all you hafta do is say you're the Social Credit man representin' Mr. Aberhart and the smiles come out as if they'd been kept in the root cellar.

**Mrs. Roothe:** Could you eat something, Albert?

**Albert:** Sure, Mom.

**Mrs. Roothe:** You're awfully thin.

**Albert:** Stop worrying.

**Mrs. Roothe:** Dougie, why don't you have a look in Babe's room while I make dinner?

*Mrs. Roothe exits.*

**Albert:** Now what's all this?

**Doug:** Nothing.

**Albert:** Doug.

**Doug:** I just . . .

**Albert:** I won't have you poking around.

**Doug:** I just wanted . . . to see.

**Albert:** See what, Doug? You can tell me what's on your mind or you can go home.

**Doug:** It's about . . . the window. The window Babe climbed out that night. You see, it's the same as my window and—

**Albert:** Dougie, Dougie . . .

**Doug:** But I think it's important. You see, there's no way that he could have opened the window from the inside. That means someone opened the window for him. Someone asked him outside and he went.

**Albert:** Doug, I appreciate your interest.

**Doug:** There's only three people Babe would crawl out the window to meet. Me, Norm, or . . . Diane Thorpe. Unless you can think of anyone else.

**Albert:** The case is closed.

**Doug:** Do you get what I'm saying? Whoever opened that window was the last person to see him alive.

**Albert:** I think you've been reading too many of those detective serials.

**Doug:** Someone opened Babe's window! It must have been Diane!

**Albert:** What is it you want, Doug? Would you like me to go to Mr. Thorpe and accuse his daughter of murder? Would that fulfill your desire for melodrama?

**Doug:** They gotta re-open the case!

**Albert:** They'll do nothing of the kind.

**Doug:** But this is new evidence!

**Albert:** There's a hundred reasons why that window might have been open. Babe might have opened it himself, the day before.

**Doug:** Your mom would have noticed, don't you think?

**Albert:** I don't want this raised in front of Mom. Now I think you better go.

**Doug:** You just don't want anything to wreck your chances in the election, do you?

*Doug tries to leave. Albert grabs him by the arm.*

**Albert:** You apologize. Right now.

**Doug:** Well it's true, isn't it?

*Albert tightens his grip on Doug's arm.*

**Albert:** Doug.

**Doug:** Okay, I'm sorry! But why don't you want to know what happened?

**Albert:** I do know what happened, Doug. I do know. Babe had a little romance with the Thorpe girl. I think things went a bit too far and Babe felt guilty. I don't think he meant to kill himself. I think maybe he got caught up in the drama of pretending he was going to kill himself and then . . . something went wrong. For once Babe got himself into something he couldn't get out of.

**Doug:** *After a long beat.* How come you never said any of this at the inquest?

**Albert:** It seemed senseless to cause any more pain. It wasn't going to bring him back.

**Doug:** You think I don't know that!? Why does everyone keep saying that?

**Albert:** Then you tell me. What's the point?

**Doug:** Just . . . to know. Just . . .

**Albert:** I see. I guess you don't find a lot of spiritual answers in your household, do you?

**Doug:** And you know the answers just 'cause you're a holy roller? You think old ratty Thorpe knows? Maybe I'll ask him—

**Albert:** You'll do nothing of the kind. Mr. Thorpe's got enough on his mind without you bothering him.

*Mrs. Roothe enters.*

**Mrs. Roothe:** I expect we could eat now.

**Doug:** I gotta go, Mrs. Roothe. Thanks for the lemonade.

**Mrs. Roothe:** What about dinner?

**Doug:** No . . . no thanks.

**Albert:** You remember what I said about helping on election day, Dougie. You might just learn something.

**Doug:** Yes, I'd like to learn something.

*Doug exits.*

**Mrs. Roothe:** Albert, what's that all about? Albert?


## SCENE 37

*Doug walks down the sidewalk past the Fetterman's. He is nearly knocked over by two moving men who emerge from the front of the house with a heavy piece of furniture.*

**Doug:** Hey . . .

**Mover:** Out of the way, son.

**Doug:** What's going on?

**Mover:** What's it look like?

*Norm emerges from the house, sniffling to himself. Pete Thorpe lurks in the background, as yet unnoticed by the boys.*

**Doug:** Norm!

**Norm:** Thorpe—he finally kicked us out—we have to leave our house! Today!

**Doug:** Are you kidding? How can he do that?

**Norm:** He's gone crazy—he yelled at my mom for half an hour about the farmers losing their crops in the hailstorm.

**Doug:** What?

**Norm:** I don't know.

*Norm shakes his head, quietly starts to sniffle.*

**Doug:** Where'll you go?

**Norm:** Calgary, I guess. I don't know what we'll eat down there.

**Doug:** Gee, Norm—this is rotten.

*Pete approaches, stares. He looks jittery, haunted.*

**Doug:** What are you looking at?

*Pete doesn't respond. Just shakes his head slowly.*

**Doug:** I said what are you lookin' at? Huh?

**Norm:** *Still sniffly.* Go away.

**Pete:** M-moving?

**Norm:** What does it look like?

**Pete:** Y-you g-going to a different ch-church?

*A slightly stunned silence.*

**Doug:** What are you talking about?

*Mr. Thorpe storms up, takes Pete by the arm.*

**Mr. Thorpe:** Stay away from there!

*Norm approaches Mr. Thorpe.*

**Norm:** *You*—you stay away! You stay away from us!

*Mr. Thorpe pulls Pete off. Pete struggles to get away.*

**Pete:** S-sorry.

**Mr. Thorpe:** Peter! Come along!

*The Thorpes exit. Movers pass by on their way back into the house.*

**Doug:** What a couple of creeps.

**Norm:** I better go—I'm supposed to be helping.

*Doug nods miserably, Norm moves off.*

## SCENE 38

*Doug approaches the Thorpe house.*

**Doug:** It seemed to me old Thorpe had single-handedly ruined my
life. Moving here with his beautiful daughter to tempt Babe,
then whisking her away to Bible college before she could be
held accountable for her actions. And now kicking my friend
out of his own house. No one should have that kind of power. I
tried to think of what Babe would have done in similar circum-
stances but I couldn't summon his cool.

I walked up to the Thorpe house composing my speech about
Diane and taxes and un-neighborly behavior. I stopped dead at
the sound of Pete Thorpe crying out in real pain, like a wound-
ed animal.

Mr. Thorpe was silhouetted in the back window, his arm raised
to hit Pete again. And again. I stood frozen for a few seconds,
watching what was no doubt a familiar scene.

I could have yelled for help. I could have thrown a few punch-
es of my own. I could have set the house on fire—maybe that
would have distracted Thorpe from the task at hand.

*Doug starts to back away, then stops, stricken.*

I ran away.


## SCENE 39

**Albert:** *Making a speech.* Just as blood must flow to every part of
the body, feeding, clothing, and sheltering every cell, so must
credit flow to every individual and his own productive enter-
prise. Nothing must be allowed to interfere with this flow of
credit.

**Doug:** Albert! Babe's dead!

**Albert:** The blood flows to every part of the body, feeding, clothing, and sheltering every cell . . .

**Doug:** He's gone. Just like that!

**Albert:** Nothing must be allowed to interfere with this flow of credit.

**Doug:** Nothing must be allowed to interfere with your campaign.

*Albert smiles at his audience.*

**Albert:** Thank you.

**Mr. Sayers:** Circumstantial evidence, Doug. Not even that.

**Doug:** What about the window?

**Mr. Sayers:** The case is closed.

**Jean:** The window is closed.

**Coroner:** We could offer no other verdict than that of suicide. So say you all?

**Chorus:** Jack Frost.

**Jean:** Put Jack Frost to rest.

**Doug:** I'm sorry, Babe. Babe!

**Coroner:** So say you all?

**Doug:** I miss you.

**Chorus:** We all do.

**Norm:** Dougie! Dougie! Our troubles are over—they put Billy in reform school! I'm not a baby!

**Doug:** Come back, Norm.


## SCENE 40

*Chorus floods onto the stage.*

**Chorus:** August 22, 1935—Election Day!

**Various:** The mobs came pouring out of the rows of tiny frame houses.

They came downstairs from back rooms over grocery stores.

They came upstairs from basements.

Truckloads of men from the relief camps rumbled through the streets.

The wooden sidewalks thundered with a clatter of heels pounding out a revolt as surely as if they had been carrying their shotguns instead of voting cards.

Before noon the polls were overwhelmed. The panic-stricken electoral officers sent out calls for more pencils, for carpenters to slap together more booths, for police to keep order.

There had never been anything like it.

Witnesses to revolution. That's what we were.


## SCENE 41

*The Sayers household. The family gathers around the radio.*

**Announcer:** And it looks like a clean sweep, with Social Credit elected in twenty-one ridings, leading in thirty-eight.

**Mr. Sayers:** Looks like a split vote in the city.

**Mrs. Sayers:** Still nothing on Albert's riding?

**Mr. Sayers:** Must be a close one then.

*Albert takes up a victory stance on top of the grandstand.*

**Announcer:** Albert Roothe, an Edmonton high-school teacher, has been declared elected for Social Credit in Strathcona-Whitemud.

**Doug:** Who cares?

**Mrs. Sayers:** Mrs. Roothe said to come over.

**Mr. Sayers:** I guess they deserve something to celebrate, don't they?

*The neighborhood gathers at the Roothe's.*

**Albert:** Tonight our prairie tract leapt to world attention. Social Credit held out an answer to the dull heresy of communism and the brutality of ascendant fascism. It was the way out.

**Doug:** No, it wasn't.

**Mr. Sayers:** On being asked when the basic dividends would be paid, Mr. Aberhart told the press: no person can say just how soon we will be ready to pay the basic dividends, because we don't know what difficulties may arise in building the new world order.

**Doug:** Things get so complicated, don't they?


## SCENE 42

*The Sayers household. Doug stares out the window. Mrs. Sayers approaches.*

**Mrs. Sayers:** Dougie?

**Doug:** What?

**Mrs. Sayers:** You look a little glum.

**Doug:** I was just . . . I wish . . . we were religious.

**Mrs. Sayers:** *Laughing.* Would you rather you'd been born into the Thorpe family, Dougie?

**Doug:** No . . .

**Mrs. Sayers:** Mrs. Roothe seemed to think you were still brooding about Babe.

**Doug:** I wish we could have gone to the funeral.

**Mrs. Sayers:** Sometimes that helps, alright. I'm sorry we're not more devout, Doug. We haven't really equipped you to deal with . . . manifestations of divine will, have we?

**Doug:** Do you think that's why it happened? Divine . . . what'd you say?

**Mrs. Sayers:** I . . . don't know.

**Doug:** Our last year's social teacher said the Depression is a . . . visitation. A punishment, a warning to humanity.

**Mrs. Sayers:** I'm sure he was speaking in economic terms, Doug. People were very greedy in the twenties, some think it might have helped cause the Depression. But sometimes . . . there is no reason.

**Doug:** *After a pause* . Right.

**Mrs. Sayers:** You okay, Doug?

*Doug nods. Mrs. Sayers exits.*

**Doug:** I wanted to go on and ask if such sweeping divine rules applied to individuals too; if it was possible that Babe had taken the ultimate punishment for having such a good time, for his mischief and bubbling ideas, for his irreverence, for being liked too much? Did this kind of careless, slouching joy in life also bring down wrath and visitations from on high? It gave one pause, and I vowed to be careful, not to enjoy life too much, or at least not to be too blatant and attract attention from Upstairs. It seemed unfair, somehow, but everyone kept saying we were victims of the Depression. Victims. And sometimes victims were sacrificed, weren't they?

**Babe:** *Gently.* Case closed, Dougie?

**Doug:** Babe . . . I wish you could come over . . .

**Babe:** Can't.

**Doug:** I know. Babe, I don't know what else to do. No one seems to care—

**Babe:** Some summer, huh, Dougie? Hot. I had to get out of here—it was so hot.

**Doug:** You're not mad?

**Babe:** Nah . . . I barely remember. And now I'm going for a nice, cold swim.

*Babe smiles gently.*

**Doug:** August 23, 1935—I gave up on you, Babe.

*Faint sound of artillery, other "war-time" noises in the background.*

**Doug:** Because . . . sometimes there is no reason.

**Babe:** Don't worry.

**Doug:** Sometimes there is no reason. Good preparation for fighting a war, I guess. Day after day of senseless slaughter. The death of hope just when people thought they'd found it. Death without meaning. Just like the Aberhart summer. *A beat.* Case closed.

*Pete appears out of the shadows.*

**Babe:** Not quite.

**Pete:** July, 1944.

**Doug:** I never told anybody, Pete. I promised I'd never tell.


## SCENE 43

**Pete:** An army hospital in the north of France.

**Doug:** I was there getting some of the shrapnel picked out of me and recovering from my head wound.

*Chorus enters and become patients. Artillery noises in the background. Doug discovers Pete.*

**Doug:** Pete? It's Doug Sayers.

**Doctor:** You know him?

**Doug:** Yes, he's an old buddy. What's wrong with him?

**Doctor:** Well for one thing, he's a non-ID. He was found in an SAR tank that'd been hit by a Panserschreck. Recovery crew found him huddled in a corner.

**Doug:** So now what?

**Doctor:** I'm not a psychiatrist. Oh, if I had some drugs, maybe a bit of shock therapy and he'd come out of it. But who's got the time?

*The Doctor exits.*

**Doug:** *To Pete.* I'm sorry, Pete. What I did to you—it was crazy, cruel. But I was half out of my head.

*The Doctor returns.*

**Doctor:** You were right. They've traced a P. J. Thorpe with an M regimental number who joined up in April, 1942. The Provost people think it could be a desertion case.

**Doug:** Desertion? No, no—I don't think so.

**Doctor:** That's what it looks like. Desertion.

**Doug:** Maybe I shouldn't have said anything.

**Doctor:** Nonsense. Go and have your dressing changed.

**Doug:** I'd like to see if I can get him to recognize me. Maybe if he'll talk he can tell me what happened.

**Doctor:** I suppose I don't see any harm in you trying. Dredge up some common memories and see what happens.

*Doctor moves off. Doug approaches Pete.*

**Doug:** Doug Sayers, Pete. Come on, it's time for your walk. Come and keep me company.

*Doug and Pete walk together.*

**Doug:** Hey, Pete . . . Pete. What's the deal? You can't talk or you won't? Huh?

*No response.*

**Doug:** Remember the old neighborhood, Pete? You remember when Headley's barn got struck by lightning? What about the hacienda ruins in the ravine, Pete? Right below Cawners' caves, remember? The day the cops raided Cawners, I remember the shots. They fired two warning shots after Neil Cawner. You remember? Were you with us when we tried to make Babe's dog smoke? Then your dad gave us a sermon about the evils of tobacco.

*Pete pulls away from Doug, starts walking back.*

**Doug:** He was a real son of a bitch, wasn't he? A real bastard. I'm sorry Pete—we were just kids. We didn't know, did we?

## SCENE 44

*Memory: The boys enter—Doug, Norm, Babe, with Pete trailing behind.*

**Pete:** The Shadow knows.

**Norm:** How'd you do that?

**Pete:** I l-listen to the radio a lot . . .

**Babe:** You got a sister, don't you?

**Pete:** *Imitating Diane.* My name is Diane Thorpe.

**Babe:** Not bad.

**Pete:** . . .You guys going into the barn?

**Babe:** Maybe.

**Doug:** Ahh, Babe . . .

**Pete:** I-I got a candle. I'll go get it.

**Babe:** Good thinking, Pete.

*Norm and Babe go into the barn. Pete won't go, refusing to follow along with the memory.*

**Doug:** We went into the barn. Your dad came out and started yelling. Remember? *Imitating Mr. Thorpe.* Peter! Come out of that barn. *As Doug.* Come on—your dad's here and he's yelling for you. Peter!

*Pete shoves Doug, tries to turn away from him. Doug hangs on.*

**Doug:** He never let you do anything, did he? He even took your radio! Why'd he do that? Come on, Pete—you can say it—he was a son of a bitch!

*Doug shoves Pete against a wall. He falls to the ground.*

**Doug:** Come on!

*Pete slowly gets up.*

**Pete:** Brother Thorpe, we have been blessed by your presence these past few weeks. You have been faithful and good in your attendance. You have a fine family. My, what a beautiful daughter, the Lord's blessing. But, if you will forgive me, I cannot help wondering why you have not arisen to testify, nor come forward during the altar call at the Mercy Seat.

**Doug:** What's that, Pete? What's the "mercy seat"?

**Pete:** *As Mr. Thorpe.* We will be moving on to another house of worship.

**Doug:** Who's that, Pete? Your dad?

**Pete:** *As Mr. Thorpe.* Peter! Come here and listen to what I have to say.

*Mr. Thorpe enters and Pete enters the scene as his younger self. Doug withdraws along with the rest of the neighborhood to watch.*

**Mr. Thorpe:** I'm going to tell you something that you may or may not completely understand.

**Pete:** W-what . . .

**Mr. Thorpe:** I know about your crystal radio set, you know. Stop your cringing. There's no punishment coming to you, only to me. I'm going to admit to you that I have failed and ask your forgiveness.

Yesterday, when you all went to the picnic, I went to the kitchen to get sandwiches from the icebox. The house was so silent with all of you gone, I began to notice the drip, drip, drip of the overflow from the melting ice, into the pan under the icebox. Afterwards, I wondered if it was a sign.

*The Chorus closes in now, listening.*

**Mr. Thorpe:** I took the pan out to the backyard and threw the water onto the grass. When I was finished, I happened to look up, and there, along the lane, I saw your sister and the boy.

**Babe:** Other stuff to do.

**Mr. Thorpe:** I stepped into the garage so they wouldn't see me. I watched as they slipped into the barn. All of my being told me to go there and drag them out, but a guiding hand seemed to touch me and hold me back. I didn't know what to do. I waited, I prayed, I asked for guidance before taking the step to include you in this struggle . . .

**Pete:** W-what d-do you mean?

**Mr. Thorpe:** All I want you to do is get the lad out alone for a talk so that I can set him straight.

**Pete:** Please . . . d-don't m-make me . . . please . . .

**Mr. Thorpe:** Son? Peter? It's only right, only fair to both of them before they do what they may regret for the rest of their lives.

**Pete:** Please, Papa . . . no . . .

**Mr. Thorpe:** Go on.

## SCENE 45

*Pete throws gravel at Babe's window to wake him up. Babe comes to the window.*

**Pete:** *In Diane's voice.* Psst, Babe? It's Diane.

**Babe:** *Stunned.* Diane?

**Pete:** Can you meet me in the barn?

**Babe:** Yeah . . . okay. I'll sneak out.

**Pete:** I already opened your window. See you in a minute?

**Babe:** Yes.


## SCENE 46

*Mr. Thorpe waits for Babe, flashlight in hand. Babe creeps into the loft.*

**Babe:** Diane? Diane, where are you?

*Babe creeps closer and closer to Mr. Thorpe until he nearly stumbles over him. Mr. Thorpe turns the flashlight on his own face, startling Babe.*

**Mr. Thorpe:** She's not here, son. Nor is she likely to be.

**Babe:** Mr. Thorpe?

**Mr. Thorpe:** Yes. I want to talk to you. I know everything.

**Babe:** What do you mean, you know everything?

**Mr. Thorpe:** I can assure you that this is not a time for lying. I saw you and Diane come in here yesterday.

**Babe:** We were just—

**Mr. Thorpe:** Quiet! I am well aware of the nature of your sin.

**Babe:** What do you mean?

**Mr. Thorpe:** I have prayed for forgiveness for my negligence as a father. Now it is time for you to pray.

**Babe:** What are you doing?

**Mr. Thorpe:** You will repent. Here. Tonight.

*Mr. Thorpe pushes Babe onto the box and wraps the rope loosely around his neck.*

**Babe:** *Terrified.* Jesus . . .

**Mr. Thorpe:** I want you to repent. But first I want you to look into the abyss.

*A long silence as they stare at each other.*

**Mr. Thorpe:** Well?

**Babe:** I . . . I'm sorry.

**Mr. Thorpe:** *Approaching Babe.* You're sorry.

**Babe:** I'm sorry Diane couldn't come out tonight.

*Mr. Thorpe lets out a roar and kicks the box out from underneath Babe. He flees. Pete sits by the door of the barn, frozen.*

**Mr. Thorpe:** Peter! Come along! Peter, get out of the barn!

*Pete stays behind as Mr. Thorpe exits.*

## SCENE 47

*Hospital grounds: Pete tries to run away, but Doug hangs on to him.*

**Doug:** Why! Why?

**Pete:** *Looking past Doug to Babe.* Jesus, you're dumb Babe. You're supposed to be the smart one, you and your big smile and your good looks. All the girls playing dead for you and you pick on Di, for Chrissake. You didn't know, did you, Babe? Why do you think he'd never go up to the Mercy Seat, why we ran around from church to church like that? He wasn't going to let you have her, or anybody else. He wanted her for himself. Didn't you know that? I knew that.

**Doug:** Oh, Jesus, Pete. No . . .

**Pete:** Here comes the altar call. Come forth and unburden yourself of your sin and your fears. Papa, why can't we go? Why do we sit here, all the others have gone forward.

**Mr. Thorpe:** *To Pete.* I meant to cut him down immediately, so he'd have nothing more than a bad rope burn on his neck. But it was too fast. All too fast. All too late.

**Pete:** Come to the Mercy Seat of God. Stand up and freely express your sin. Accept the salvation that only He can bestow.

*The rest of the Chorus draws closer.*

**Doug:** The window, Pete—right under my nose all that time. And Thorpe . . . I can only imagine . . .

**Mr. Thorpe:** What a beautiful daughter—the Lord's blessing. Every day I felt like I was being choked, strangled. I could hardly breathe. But the Lord knows I won the struggle— driving desire back down into the earth, like grounding a dangerous electrical current.

**Jean:** Something had to give.

**Doug:** *To Thorpe.* He was fifteen. He was the world to us.

**Mr. Thorpe:** I meant to cut him down immediately. I meant to. But maybe something, someone had to be . . . sacrificed.

**Albert:** Babe—reaching out of doorways, trying to catch me. After he died, the dream stopped.

**Mr. Thorpe:** After he died, I sent Diane away. I sent away the Lord's blessing.

**Doug:** Babe was the blessing—

**Albert:** Once I stopped having the dream, I knew it was a sign. A sign that it was going to be my summer.

**Doug:** Albert?

**Albert:** Just for a moment, there was a feeling of relief. About

Babe. It lasted for one single instant but it was . . . unforgivable. It made me work harder, pray harder, speak louder, longer—I carried the word into every dark corner that summer. I felt as though I'd sacrificed my brother . . . he was the price paid for winning—

**Doug:** Albert elected and Babe dead—

**Coroner:** A careless slouching joy in life. Hope.

**Jean:** Something had to give—

**Mrs. Fetterman:** Like the weather—I thought the sky was falling—

**Jean:** Like the war.

**Albert:** I was carrying the word—

**Pete:** Desire—

**Albert:** Hope!

**Mr. Thorpe:** Too fast—too late!

**Pete:** Dougie.

**Doug:** Hope.

*An explosion.*

**Doug:** January, 1945. A bomb lands in a grove of poplars at the far end of the hospital. The entire wing where Pete is collapses. Pete Thorpe disappeared forever—no body, no tags, no trace. I sometimes wonder if he walked away from the rubble and has been wandering around Europe ever since, curling up nights in culverts and ditches.

*Chorus disperses, leaving only Pete and Doug.*

**Pete:** *To Doug.* Come to the Mercy Seat.

**Doug:** Me.

*Pete holds Doug's gaze for a few moments, then exits.*

**Doug:** Did you ever think maybe we're all destined to be responsible for one other person? A person bonded to us by an obligation we don't even understand until we've failed? I'm sorry, Pete . . .

*Doug starts to leave.*

I walk by the Thorpe place on the way to my car. A curtain drops back into place, as if someone didn't want to get caught looking at me. I open the car door but can't leave without one last glance back. Still looking for . . . a baseball mitt, a precious memory, a musty stash of hope? All lost that summer.

That was a long time ago, though, and I'm alright now.

*Curtain.*